The
Wright
Brothers

The Wright Brothers

RICHARD M. HAYNES

Silver Burdett Press, Inc.

To my Dianne. 1–4–3–4

CONSULTANTS:

Robert M. Goldberg
Consultant to the Social Studies Department
(formerly Department Chair)
Oceanside Middle School
Oceanside, New York

Michael Kort
Associate Professor
Boston University

AUTHOR'S ACKNOWLEDGMENTS:
Special thanks to Dr. Tom Crouch, Curator of Aeronautics, and Dr. Peter Jakab,
historian, with the Air and Space Museum of the Smithsonian Institution in
Washington, D.C., and to the staffs of both the Library of Congress and the Wright
State University Archives, Wright Collections, for their time and assistance.

PHOTOGRAPH AND DIAGRAM ACKNOWLEDGMENTS:
Smithsonian Institution: 13, 19, 31, 34, 35, 75, 81, 88–89, 124–125, 134, 135; Wright
State University: 2, 12, 17, 65, 66, 90, 118, 121, 132, 135.

SERIES AND COVER DESIGN:
R STUDIO T Raúl Rodríguez and Rebecca Tachna

PHOTO RESEARCH:
Omni-Photo Communications, Inc.

Published by Silver Burdett Press, Inc., a division of Simon & Schuster, Inc.,
Englewood Cliffs, NJ 07632.

Library of Congress Cataloging-in-Publication Data

Haynes, Richard M.
The Wright brothers / Richard M. Haynes.
p. cm.—(Pioneers in change)
Includes bibliographical references and index.
Summary: Traces the lives of the Wright brothers and describes how
they showed the world how to fly.
1. Wright, Orville, 1871–1948—Juvenile literature.
2. Wright, Wilbur, 1867–1912—Juvenile literature.
3. Aeronautics—United States—Biography—Juvenile literature.
[1. Wright, Orville, 1871–1948.   2. Wright, Wilbur, 1867–1912.
3. Aeronautics—Biography.]   I. Title.   II. Series.
TL540.W7H39   1991
629.13'0092'2—dc20
[B]   91-9195
                                                                      CIP
                                                                      AC

Manufactured in the United States of America.
ISBN 0-382-24168-1   [lib. bdg.]
10 9 8 7 6 5 4 3 2 1
ISBN 0-382-24175-4 [pbk.]
10 9 8 7 6 5 4 3 2 1

CONTENTS

1

7 Hawthorn Street

Orville and Wilbur Wright taught the world how to do something that people had been trying to do since ancient times. The idea that people, too, could soar like the birds in the air had captured the imagination of men and women everywhere. Many of the greatest minds in history had wrestled with the problem of making this idea a reality. But it was the Wright brothers who finally unlocked the secrets of flight. The two brothers had never even graduated from high school. Neither one ever married nor left their parents' home. One wanted to be a teacher, the other a printer. They were shy men who didn't want the world's attention. Why would two such unlikely men succeed where so many others had failed? Perhaps the answer can be found in the family from which they came.

The person who had the greatest influence on both

Orville and Wilbur was their father. His name was Milton Wright, and he was raised in a strict and conservative home in which he learned the values of family, religion, and education. It was young Milton's father, Dan, who seems to have shaped him the most. Milton was the second of three brothers. All of them had a strong resemblance to their father—from the not tall but light build to the eyes that were so full of life. Dan Wright didn't belong to a particular church, but he was a keen reader of the Bible. It was this reading of "the good book" that had taught him morals and a love of family. The Wright family had moved from Ohio to the edge of the Indiana wilderness. During the 1830s life on the frontier was a struggle. But Dan had been well educated, and he was determined that his children would be, too.

Milton's mother, Catherine, left practically no written records of her life. It is known that Milton adored her and that they were very close. He said it was she who really taught him the religion that would be his life's work. Like his brothers, Milton had decided to become a minister. However, his oldest brother died when he was young. Then his younger brother became ill and could not live an active life. The family name now rested on Milton.

It wasn't unusual to find small churches on the frontier that didn't follow the teachings of major religions. One of these small groups was the Church of the United Brethren in Christ. It was a conservative and strict church whose members read the Bible daily and believed its every word. This was the church that Milton belonged to. By age twenty-four he had been a presiding elder and then became a full minister in the church. In 1853 it was not unusual that a person was not paid for such a church position. To earn a living, therefore, Milton had been working as a teacher in small local frontier schools since 1849. The work was hard but rewarding, and he loved it. He was truly happy when he succeeded with a struggling student. He had had only one year of college training, but this was far more than most people on the frontier had received. It was natural that he should become a teacher.

Milton had attended Hartsville College, which was run by the United Brethren Church. The year he spent there strengthened his religious beliefs and his devotion to the family. It was during the year at Hartsville College that Milton met Susan Koerner. Susan turned twenty-two that year. Her parents, John and Catherine, had left Virginia when she was only eighteen months old. They bought 170 acres of good land to farm on the Indiana frontier near Richmond. Shortly after arriving, the Koerners became members of the United Brethren Church.

Susan's father had been the guiding force in her life. John Koerner was an active member of the church, and his daughter followed this example. He was also good with his hands and could fix almost anything mechanical. Susan, too, had this gift. She was very bright, and her father believed in education. As a result, Susan was sent to Hartsville College. Sending young women to college was almost unheard-of at this time.

The year 1853 was the only one Milton and Susan spent in school together. He was anything but mechanical, and she was terribly shy. But they shared their faith and a belief in the importance of family. Milton didn't return to Hartsville the following year because he had taken a job as a circuit minister for the church. Milton's job as a circuit minister took him to many small churches that were spread out across the frontier. Because he and others like him would preach at one church and ride on to the next,

9

they were also called circuit riders. Movement from one place to another never ended. This became the pattern of Milton's life of service to the church.

By 1857 Milton had been assigned a new ministry in Oregon. In those days the best way to get from Indiana to Oregon was by going to the East Coast, boarding a ship, and sailing south all the way around South America and then back north along the Pacific coast. Milton and Susan had become a couple by then, and he had asked her to marry him. But Susan wanted to wait until his work in Oregon was finished.

This waiting period stretched over a full two and a half years. When Milton returned to Indiana in 1859, the clouds of civil war between the North and the South were growing. But Milton was tired of waiting. On Thanksgiving Day, 1859, he and Susan were married. By then he was thirty, and she was twenty-eight. But they understood each other and the family roles they were to play. Even though she had been well educated, Susan felt that a woman's place was in the home. The shy bride looked forward to bringing up her children and filling theirs and her husband's days with good food and happiness. She and Milton were united in this belief in the family. She also believed firmly in doing whatever Milton's job required them to do. Like their parents before them, Milton and Susan would teach their children the same values they themselves had been taught.

There were many moves for the young couple during those early years. Milton had to give up the teaching he so loved to take a church circuit elsewhere in Indiana. It wasn't an easy thing to do, but they went willingly. On March 17, 1861, the first of several children was born to Milton and Susan Wright. They named their oldest son

Reuchlin. On November 11, 1862, less than a year and a half later, Susan gave birth to another son. They named him Lorin. The family of four lived quietly on the frontier while the greatest war in American history, the Civil War, raged far to the east and south.

When the Civil War ended, Milton bought his family a farm near New Castle, Indiana. It was here that the Wrights' third son, Wilbur Fiske, was born on April 16, 1867. The money Milton earned from the small farm and from preaching wasn't great, but he and Susan still managed to create a warm and loving home. When Wilbur was barely a year old, service to the church called Milton to teaching again. The family moved so that he could accept the position of professor of religion at the United Brethren School. These were tense times for the tiny church group because there were many disagreements among the leaders. Milton Wright was a man who expressed his beliefs openly. As a result, he soon found himself in the middle of a storm of church disagreements. He would be in such a position many times throughout his busy life. But his ability to speak, think, and write clearly also brought him the rewards of leadership. He soon became editor of the church newspaper, the *Religious Telescope*. Although this was quite an honor, the family had to move yet again.

This move took the Wrights to Dayton, Ohio, where they rented a house in June 1869. Life in quiet Dayton was a bit more settled than it had been in farm country. Susan, never a strong woman, was expecting another baby. This time she delivered twins, Ida and Otis. But Ida died at birth, and Otis died about a month later. During the 1870s death among infants was very common, but the parents never forgot the children they lost this way.

It was time for another change. Milton Wright began

11

Susan Koerner Wright in about 1870. She had a strong religious faith and a firm belief in the importance of family.

The Wright family home at 7 Hawthorn Street in West Dayton, Ohio. This photograph was taken in 1900.

to look for a more permanent home for his family. For $1,800 he bought a small, brand-new house at 7 Hawthorn Street in West Dayton, which was separated from Dayton by the Miami River. It was a small but growing area of working-class homes. The streets were quiet and tree-lined. The small house sat on a very narrow lot among a row of houses much like itself. The people who lived in this neighborhood tended to work in Dayton and then return home to their families in West Dayton. It was a good place in which to raise children. Hawthorn Street really became home.

Shortly after this move, Susan became pregnant again.

On August 19, 1871, she gave birth to her last son—Orville Dewey. He wouldn't be her last child, however. Three years later, on the same date in August, she did have her last child. The Wrights' only daughter, Katharine, was born when Susan Wright was forty-three. Now the happy father of five children, Milton Wright prided himself on teaching all of his children the first *McGuffey's Reader* before they even went to school. This was one of a series of school-books that were widely used in those days. (In fact, they are still available today.) As the only girl and the youngest child, Katharine sometimes had a hard time with so many rough older brothers around her. But so did Orville. His best friend, Ed Sines, lived just down the street. When Orville was five years old, his mother proudly walked him to kindergarten on his first day. After that, he was expected to go without her. It took a while for her to find out that Orville had not gone back to school after that first day. It seems that he and Ed had been having fun together—all day long! Of course, Susan Wright didn't approve of this kind of behavior. She decided to teach Orville at home.

The Wrights were a very close family. Milton and Susan Wright were strict parents, as their parents had been with them. But they were also warm and loving. The two oldest boys, Reuchlin and Lorin, were close in age and interests. They became a natural pair. Wilbur, who was in the middle, wanted to follow the older boys. But the four and a half years that separated them made this difficult. The age difference between Wilbur and Orville was the same as that between Wilbur and the older boys. While he loved his little sister, Orville always spent more time with his older brother. As for Wilbur, he really seemed to enjoy the role of being older and wiser. It was a role he never gave up. The family had nicknames for everyone. Wilbur was either Will or "Ullam." Orville was called Orv as well as "Bubbo." And Katharine was "Swes." At times even the strict "Father" gave way to a loving "Pop."

By now Milton Wright found that he was increasingly being called away on church business. As editor of the *Religious Telescope,* his ideas and beliefs attracted the attention of many people. It therefore came as no surprise when the church honored him by electing him bishop in 1877. But with added honors came added duty. Another move loomed ahead.

2

"I Was a Good Boy Today"

In 1878 Wilbur was eleven years old, and Orville was seven. That was the year Bishop Wright moved his family to Cedar Rapids, Iowa. Perhaps the family sensed that they would never really leave the Dayton area, because they didn't sell the Hawthorn Street house. It was rented while they were gone. Cedar Rapids wasn't called home for very long, though. Soon it was necessary to move to Adair, Iowa, where another new home was bought. With the younger boys in school, these were very important years for the Wright children. The family adjusted well with each move.

The bishop's travels became more frequent. But he wrote home often and expected to hear from everyone. This pattern of letter writing among the Wrights would continue throughout the years. Because the family saved many of these letters—and there were hundreds of them

Wilbur Wright in 1878.

17

over the years—historians have a clear picture of the Wrights' family life. Among the earliest of these letters is a one-cent postcard from ten-year-old Orville. It reads:

Cedar Rapids Town   Apr 1881 [April 11, 1881]
Dear Father
I got your letter today. My teacher said I was a good boy today. We have 45 in our room. The other day I took a machine can and filled it with water then I put it on the stove. I waited a little while and the water came squirting out of the top about a foot. The water in the river was up in the cracker factory about a half a foot. There is a good deal water on the Island. The old cat is dead.

Your son Orville

This postcard tells quite a bit about the Wrights. It shows how active young Orville's mind was and how sharp his powers of observation were. That "machine can" must have made a mess of Susan Wright's stove. But the children were all encouraged to explore, to think things through, and to try out their ideas. Orville would be the most mechanically minded of all the sons. He got that from his mother, who, it is said, could fix almost anything.

Bishop Wright expected his children to experiment with things, but he also expected them to earn their own money for these experiments. They were free to spend whatever they earned on themselves. He taught his sons that all they needed was enough money to support themselves without having to rely on anyone else. The bishop taught by example. His many letters home were supplemented by a diary he wrote in every day. Since he had been

Orville Wright in 1878.

a schoolteacher and was both an editor and a writer, he expected his children to be able to write well. He therefore filled his home with books, including at least two sets of encyclopedias. These books had been bought for the children as well as for the adults. To the bishop's delight, his children had an endless curiosity. He fed this curiosity by providing them with enough books to take them wherever they wanted to go. Reflecting on his childhood, Orville explained his father's influence: "If my father had not been the kind who encouraged his children to pursue intellectual interests without any thought of profit, our early curiosity about flying would have been nipped too early to bear fruit."

Like many parents, Bishop Wright sometimes brought small gifts to his children when he returned from a business trip. He enjoyed looking for toys that were both unusual and educational. From one of these trips he took when the boys were young, he brought home a toy that had been popular in Europe for hundreds of years. It was a toy "helicopter" with a rubber-band–windup motor. When he tossed the helicopter into the air, the boys were fascinated by it. But they weren't content to just watch it fly. Soon they were busy making their own models of the toy. But the boys couldn't help noticing that the bigger the model, the less steady it was in flight. Perhaps that was why it had never been made into more than a toy. This may have been the beginning of the Wright boys' interest in flight.

At this time both Wilbur and Orville were fairly good students. Orville won a penmanship award and was a dedicated reader. His keen mind allowed him to memorize, word for word, much of what he read. He was the outgoing one. Wilbur was quieter, always thinking but saying little. He especially loved history and geography.

By 1881 church problems again forced the family to move. This time Milton Wright's outspoken ways kept him from being reelected bishop. He decided to accept a circuit church appointment near Richmond, Indiana. The move proved to be a pleasant one for Susan Wright and the children because it brought them close to her parents' farm. They visited often, and the farm was a wonderful place for Orville and Wilbur to roam and explore. In one barn they found a lathe, which is a machine that holds wood while turning it so a worker with sharp tools can shape the wood. Things like wooden table legs are turned on a lathe. Perhaps Grandfather Koerner showed them how to use it. Before long the boys had built their own lathe at home. That was quite an accomplishment for two boys who weren't even sixteen years old yet. But no one in the family was surprised. The two brothers had always had this rare ability to re-create almost anything that caught their fancy. While the family lived in Richmond, Orville and Wilbur discovered *Century Magazine,* known for its beautiful woodcut prints. Orville found them fascinating and became interested in printing as a result. But he found that he couldn't make his own type!

By now Milton Wright had taken over publication of the *Richmond Star* in addition to his ministry. Money was tight in those days, but education had always been important to the Wrights. Reuchlin, the oldest, was ready for college. He was sent to Hartsville College, where his parents had been students. Lorin, only a year younger, joined him there the following year. But graduating wasn't necessarily expected in those days, so they both quit and returned to Dayton. There they took whatever jobs they could find. By 1883 Wilbur was a high school senior. He was studying demanding courses such as Greek and Latin.

Basically an A student, he was also athletic. He loved the high-wheel bicycle he had bought with his own money. Wilbur also worked with his father at the *Star,* where he maintained the machines that printed the paper. Orville, who was too young to do this type of work, often built kites and sold them to his friends.

Life for the Wright family had settled into a comfortable routine when they discovered that they would have to leave Indiana and move back to Dayton, Ohio. Everything happened so suddenly that they couldn't even wait for Wilbur to graduate from high school. Milton Wright was again being called to active service in the church. By July 1885 he had stopped publishing the *Star* and had started the *Christian Conservator.* Reuchlin, who had always been most removed from the close family, married and moved away. The following year Lorin left, but he would be back. In the meantime, Wilbur enrolled at Dayton's Central High School. He was such a good student that his parents were thinking of sending him to Yale University. He also played football that year.

Orville, on the other hand, was full of mischief. He was now in the ninth grade, but he was far from being the model student that Wilbur had always been. He only made a 79 in Latin and an 86 in algebra. He just couldn't seem to use his good mind on schoolwork. For Orville, coming back to Dayton meant picking up with his old friend, Ed Sines, who had a rubber-type printing press. Naturally, Orville was thrilled. But they soon outgrew it and invested two dollars on a bigger set. Milton Wright helped by giving his son twenty-five pounds of old metal type. Soon the boys were printing a little school newspaper they called *The Midget.* That led to taking in small printing jobs under the name "Sines and Wright."

That winter Wilbur was playing a game with friends on a frozen pond when he was accidentally struck in the head with a bat. He seemed to be all right, but a few weeks later he began to have heart flutters. Soon he was worried about his health. Plans for graduation and Yale had to be put aside. Wilbur became even quieter than he had been. Susan Wright, too, was ill. She had fought tuberculosis for some time and was growing weaker. This disease, which was called consumption in those days, destroys the lungs. There was no cure for it then. Wilbur stayed home to nurse his mother, since Milton Wright's business trips continued to take him away from home for long periods. During this time, Susan and her son developed a stronger bond.

It would take Wilbur three years to recover his health. But he spent his time reading all the books in his father's library. Soon he had joined his father in fighting for the issues that continued to divide the United Brethren Church. He even wrote his own pamphlet, surprising his father with how well he could think and express himself. Milton Wright made no secret of his desire for Wilbur to follow him into the ministry.

During this time Orville went to high school and worked at a local print shop during the summer. He did this for two years, then went on to a printing press of his own. To make this press he used a damaged slab that was to have become a tombstone. Wilbur helped him with this project. It seemed perfectly natural for the two brothers to join forces in this way—Wilbur the writer and editor, and Orville the printer. They began by printing one of Wilbur's pamphlets, and soon Wright Bros.: Job Printers had been created. Orville had already bought Ed Sines out, but Sines went to work for the Wright brothers as the business grew. No one was surprised when Orville decided not to go back to high school. In those days many people were self-taught, and graduating from school wasn't considered to be as important as it is today.

In 1888 the brothers built a bigger press that could print 500 sheets an hour. They later improved it to increase the speed. The press was now large enough to print two full-page spreads of the *Conservator*. It was quite an accomplishment for two young men. In the spring of 1889 Orville and Wilbur began to print the *West Side News* once a week. Needing more room, they rented a shop on West Third Street, just around the corner from their home at 7 Hawthorn Street. The paper listed Wilbur as the editor and Orville as the printer and publisher. But 1889 wasn't a good year in the Wright household. Susan Wright had been growing weaker. Yet she refused to have her husband called away from the church business that took him so far from home. Besides, Wilbur was there to care of her. Apart from making his mother comfortable, there was little Wilbur could do. She died on the Fourth of July in the same room where Orville had been born. Milton Wright, his heart broken with the loss of his wife, bought space for her to be buried in Woodland Cemetery. There would be enough room for the other members of the family to join her.

The family took stock of itself. Lorin, shocked by his mother's death, came home for a while. Wilbur, twenty-two by now, still lived at home. Orville, nearly eighteen, hadn't finished high school. Katharine would try to take her mother's place for her father and brothers. She was an excellent student, however, and college lay ahead for her. Life had to go on. The following year Orville and Wilbur worked to develop the *Evening Item* as a daily newspaper. But Dayton then had a total of twelve newspapers competing for readers, and the *Item* was soon discontinued. The brothers' efforts hadn't been wasted, however. From it the Wright & Wright printing plant was started.

By now Milton Wright had returned to his work in the church, with all the disagreements that kept him so busy. The household at 7 Hawthorn Street was now made up of Milton, his two youngest but grown sons, and a growing daughter. The family was now smaller than it had been, but the members had lost none of the love that had always bound them together. As the decade ended, the young men were ready for change in the 1890s.

CHAPTER

3

The Safety Bicycle

The winds of change swept across the United States as the 1890s started. This would prove to be a decade of contrasts. Often called the Gay Nineties, this decade would be one of great economic changes. For many American workers times were tough. Factory workers and farmers found the mid-1890s especially hard. Yet the later 1890s were a time of prosperity. Many new inventions and ideas developed throughout this decade. The Wright brothers were eagerly involved in these new developments.

Wilbur and Orville had achieved some success in the printing business. What they needed, however, was a good challenge. They were good at filling the orders for the small printing jobs they did. They had also had some success publishing newspapers, but everything had become a routine. They constantly found themselves thinking that there had to be more to life than this. It was almost as if the Wright brothers were one person in two bodies. Wilbur, the solemn intellectual, was often quiet. Yet Orville, the active one, often seemed to do what Wilbur was thinking. Together they were born inventors. It wasn't possible for them to be satisfied with doing the same thing over and over again for the rest of their lives.

The Wright brothers were restless at a time when the country, too, was restless. The decade of the 1890s brought with it new scientific ways of doing things. Newspapers and magazines were filled with stories about new forms of transportation. There were many more railroads now than there had been. Some of them even ran underground and through tunnels. Horses no longer offered the only means of moving people and supplies on land. The idea of a buggy that ran on a gas engine was actually being talked about. Even quiet Dayton, Ohio, was changing.

These changes didn't all occur at the same time, of course. One of them came in the form of a bicycle. Bicycles had been in use for many years. The word *bicycle* meant "two cycles." Two thin wheels had been put together and were connected by a metal frame. Since 1871 bicycles had a very large wheel in the front and a much smaller one in the back so they were called "high-wheelers." The rider sat between the wheels and pedaled from high above the ground. Balance was very important because the rider could get hurt if he or she fell—and it wasn't easy to get back on the bicycle either. Then the idea of the "safety" bicycle was introduced in England in 1879. It had two wheels of the same size, making it both safer and easier to ride. The rider's feet could now touch the ground. The first safety bicycle made its appearance in the United States in 1887. It was an instant hit.

By the beginning of the 1890s, these new bicycles had begun to appear in Dayton. Always eager to try something new, Orville was the first of the brothers to buy one. The new bikes had many features that made them better than the old ones. They used chain drive, for example, and had air-filled rubber tires, ball bearings, and even a comfortable seat. It was a far cry from the "bone shaker," the wooden-wheeled bicycle of the 1860s. But these new bicycles were also expensive. Orville spent $160 to buy a brand-new Columbia bicycle! That was a lot of money in those days, but he loved it. Wilbur, always more cautious, watched his brother for six months. Then he decided to buy a used Columbia bicycle for $80.

The bicycles gave the brothers a new excitement to share. They both loved to ride, and the town of Dayton was excellent for this. Orville was the more athletic of the two, however, and soon he began to take part in bicycle races. In the early 1890s Orville even won a few of these races. Other people liked to use the new bicycles to go on trips. They could travel as far as fifteen or twenty miles away on these new safety bikes. That's what Wilbur liked. It was more peaceful than racing, and the brothers could talk along the way. Such trips were a good way to spend the quiet summer of 1892.

It was only a matter of time before Orv and Will, as they called each other, realized that a business could be made from their new interest. After all, bicycle shops had already begun to appear in downtown Dayton, across the Miami River from Hawthorn Street. There were a dozen shops there, but the Wright brothers could open the first one in West Dayton, where they lived. So the brothers began to plan the opening of a repair and sales shop. Fixing bicycles would be a more steady business than what they had been doing, they decided. Also, this new vehicle was becoming such a craze that they might even make some money selling it. The people who worked in Dayton but lived in West Dayton could use their bicycles to get to and from work.

It was the fall of 1892, and the brothers had a great deal to do before they would be able to open their shop. But before they could get their plans into action, Wilbur suddenly fell ill. The doctor said it was his appendix and that could be dangerous. Doctors still weren't always able to tell just how serious a medical problem was. Besides, surgery was very risky because putting people to sleep for an operation was still new. The Wright family discussed what should be done. They decided to follow the doctor's suggestion and allow Wilbur's body to heal itself. Once again Wilbur found himself at home, getting over a health problem. But what really mattered to Orville was that Will did get over it! Katharine and Orville were both close to their older brother, and they took turns caring for him.

By the beginning of the Christmas season, it became clear that Wilbur was recovering. Plans for the bicycle shop could go on. Full of plans again, the brothers rented a store on West Third Street. The following spring they opened the Wright Cycle Exchange. They had decided to hold on to the print shop, so they now had two businesses to run. The bicycles they offered for sale were of top quality, as was their repair work. The brothers were known to be honest, respected cycle businessmen. Their business grew along with the popularity of bicycles. Before long they had outgrown their little shop and had to move to a larger space.

By now the printing business had been overshadowed by the brothers' growing bicycle business. They were devoting all of their time to this new business, and Ed Sines needed help with the print shop. Their older brother, Lorin, had moved back to Dayton with his family. Wilbur and Orville hired him to help Ed with the print shop. This allowed Lorin and his family to live in West Dayton, close to the old home on Hawthorn Street.

The summer of 1893 was a good one for the Wright brothers. They were repairing, selling, and renting bicycles, and Lorin's children were always available for a hug. That summer Wilbur and Orville went to Chicago and the World's Columbian Exposition, as the 1893 Chicago World's Fair was called. There they saw new inventions and ideas from many places around the world. It was a wondrous experience for the two young men. At ages twenty-six and twenty-three, they had rarely allowed themselves the luxury of a vacation. But this had been well worth it.

Orv and Will weren't content to just sell and fix bicycles. After all, they knew how the machines worked and how to make them better. As 1894 approached, they began to think about making bicycles as well as repairing and selling them. They had already renamed their company the Wright Cycle Company, and making bicycles now seemed the natural thing to do. Of course, the bicycle business was best when the weather was nice. Dayton had a fair climate, but winter was cold and hard on bicycle riders. As a result, most of their repair work had to be done during the warm months. The brothers were never at a loss for a good idea, though. Before long they had managed to tie their interest in bikes to printing and writing by starting a small weekly paper called *Snap-Shots at Current Events*. This new publication was directed at bicycle enthusiasts. The paper gave the brothers something to do during the winter months, but it didn't last long.

The Wright brothers' bicycle shop. In the twentieth century, it was moved to the Henry Ford Museum and Greenfield Village in Dearborn, Michigan, where this photograph was taken.

The slack business of fall and winter took its financial toll. Before they could start the business of making bicycles, Orv and Will needed a small loan to set up the machine shop. Like many young men, when they needed money it was to their father that they turned. Since Milton Wright still traveled a great deal, Wilbur wrote to him in September 1894:

The bicycle business is fair. Selling new wheels is about done for this year but the repairing business is good and we are getting about $20 a month from the

rent of three wheels. . . . We have done so well renting
them . . . although we really need the money invested
in them. Could you let us have about $150 for a while?
We think we could have it nearly all ready to pay back
by the time you get home.

It took Milton Wright only three days to reply: "I received
your letter. . . . I will loan you boys the $150 you ask."

Another letter that Wilbur wrote indicates that he had
more on his mind than just making bicycles, however. He
wrote to his father:

I have been thinking for some time about the advisa-
bility of taking a college course. I have thought about
it more or less for a number of years but my health has
been such that I was afraid that it might be time and
money wasted to do so. . . . I do not think I am specially
fitted for success in any commercial pursuit. . . . I
might make a living but I doubt whether I could ever
do much more than this. Intellectual effort is a pleasure for me and I think I would be better fitted for
reasonable success in some of the professions than in
business.

I have always thought I would like to be a teacher.
Although there is no hope of attaining such financial
success as might be attained in some of the other
professions, or in commercial pursuits, yet it is an
honorable pursuit, the pay is sufficient to enable me
to live comfortably and happily, and it is less subject
to uncertainties than almost any other occupation. It
would be congenial to my taste, and I think with
proper training I could be reasonably successful.

Milton Wright had always dreamed of having one of his sons follow him in his profession. It must have seemed strange to him to get this letter from Wilbur, since he himself had been a teacher before turning to the ministry. He wrote back to his middle child:

Yes, I will help you what I can in a collegiate course. I do not think a commercial life will suit you well. Probably you may not be able to go through college without some intermissions.

But going to college would take Wilbur away from the business with Orville and from his family. Katharine was already a student at Oberlin College, and perhaps that was enough. Will never did take his father up on the offer to help him with college. Instead, he turned his attention to the business of making bicycles.

The idea of manufacturing bicycles had been considered by many Americans at this time. As a result, there were many of these businesses around the country. What Wilbur and Orville needed were machines they understood. The old lathe they had copied from their grandfather's farm years earlier finally gave way to a new one. They added a drill press and a tube cutter. To save money, they moved the bicycle business into the back part of their printing company. The best time to build bicycles was during the slow winter months. The brothers set to work designing and building their own brand of bicycle. When they finished, they had a real beauty to show for their labors. They called it the Van Cleve, named for an ancestor who had been killed by Indians. The Wright Cycle Company sold the Van Cleve for $100. It showed how well the

Orville and Wilbur's father, Milton Wright, in a photograph taken about six years after his wife's death.

An 1897 photograph of Orville Wright (on the right) and Ed Sines working in the bicycle shop.

brothers worked when they could produce something that required both their hands and their minds to work together. In all, the Wright brothers made and sold about 300 bicycles.

While Wilbur and Orville enjoyed their new business and had even brought Ed Sines into it, they could see that Dayton was changing. This change was part of a revolution in transportation, and it was spreading. There was already an electric rail system connecting Dayton to Springfield, Ohio, twenty-nine miles away. Then, in 1896, a fellow mechanic and tinkerer named Cord Ruse built a gasoline-powered carriage. It was the first automobile the Wright brothers had ever seen. Imagine the noise this homemade buggy made on the quiet streets of West Dayton. Orville, ever the adventurer, loved it. Wilbur, however, wasn't impressed. Somehow, the automobile didn't impress them the way bicycles had.

Another mechanic did something similar in Detroit, Michigan, at about the same time. His name was Henry Ford, and he had built a one-cylinder gasoline engine in 1893. By 1896 he had built a two-cylinder engine onto a light carriage. This became Ford's first car. He called it his quadricycle, giving it a link with the popular bicycle. Henry Ford didn't invent the automobile. But he was one of those whose new ideas were taking root everywhere during the 1890s.

Actually, gasoline engines had been invented in Europe during the 1860s. By 1863 there were a few gasoline-powered vehicles. By 1890 there were actually a few automobile manufacturers in Europe. The first American company, however, didn't open until 1895. This was also the year that the first automobile race was held in this country. The race was from Chicago to Evanston, Illinois, on Thanksgiving Day. Thanks to a blizzard, the fifty-four-mile race took eight hours! With the race so close to Dayton, the Wright brothers were certain to read about it.

Somehow the automobile craze passed the Wright brothers by. Perhaps what happened at the end of the summer of 1896 had something to do with this. Sickness again struck the Wright family. This time it was Orville's turn. He came down with typhoid fever, which comes from infected food or water. Diseases like this were common during the 1890s, and they often killed their victims. For a while, Orville was seriously ill. For six weeks he lay delirious from the raging fever. But he was twenty-five and had youth and strength on his side. Of course, tender care from Wilbur and Katharine also helped. Lorin's children may also have helped Orville to recover. Having their brother's children close by allowed Orv and Will to enjoy a home filled with warmth and laughter. It was becoming likely that the two brothers would never marry and have children of their own. There seemed to be no room in their lives for these things. Their work was important to them. When they worked together, as they always did, they were content.

There are many stories about how Wilbur cared for his younger brother during his bout with typhoid fever. There are so many stories, in fact, that it is difficult to tell which are true. But there was something in the newspapers around the time of Orville's illness that Wilbur might have read to Orville while he recovered.

This news started in Germany, where much of the work on automobiles had begun. This time, however, there was something truly sensational going on there. It involved the idea of people flying. If people could replace horses and carriages with automobiles, what else could they do? Could they, perhaps, fly as the birds did? People had dreamed of doing this since the time of the early Greeks. There were many men who were trying to take advantage of the new technology of the 1890s. Transportation on the ground by horse and wagon gave way to railroads, electric power, and gasoline engines. Among those who tried to travel in the air was Otto Lilienthal. He was a dashing German who wanted to fly.

Otto Lilienthal was only one of the many people who were trying to fly. But he seemed to be more successful than the others in his early attempts. One of the leading scientists in the United States was Samuel Langley, who was also secretary of the Smithsonian Institution in Washington, D.C. Langley, among others, had to be shown that people could fly. Attempts to fly had been made at various times since 1891. Langley studied and reported on these efforts, so it is natural that Langley would report on the German's efforts.

Lilienthal started his attempts to fly by gliding in the air with a large kite. The newspapers of the mid-1890s loved to carry stories about his successes because they made such interesting reading. By 1896 he had completed nearly two thousand successful glides. But on August 9, 1896, Otto Lilienthal lifted off on a routine glide that ended by plunging him to his death. He had risen to a height of fifty feet when something went wrong and the glider fell earthward. Lilienthal fell to his death. The American press was filled with stories about what happened to the "flying man," as he was called. No one really knows whether Wilbur read these stories aloud while he nursed Orville back to health. But it certainly is possible. In any case, Orville slowly recovered full health and returned to the business of making bicycles.

But the days of the bicycle craze were passing, and competition was fierce. Because of Orville's illness and so much competition, the Wrights limited their business to making and repairing bicycles. The brothers again found themselves with time on their hands—time in which to dream about what incredible things machines could do. They also began to spend more time reading about Otto

Lilienthal and the other "flying men" of the day. They then turned to the Dayton Public Library to see what information on flying was available. These dedicated readers soon exhausted the library's resources. Wilbur then wrote to Samuel Langley at the Smithsonian Institution. This would be the first of hundreds of letters from the Wright brothers to the famous scientist:

> I have been interested in the problem of mechanical and human flight ever since as a boy I constructed a number of bats [as helicopters were then called] of various sizes. . . . My observations since have only convinced me more firmly that human flight is possible and practical. It is only a question of knowledge and skill. . . . I believe that simple flight at least is possible to man.

Even as he wrote this letter, Wilbur must have realized how unusual it was for an unknown bicycle maker from Ohio to say such things. But he wanted to know more. His letter continued:

> I wish to obtain such papers as the Smithsonian Institution has published on this subject. . . . I am an enthusiast, but not a crank in the sense that I have some pet theories as to the proper construction of a flying machine.

The letter was dated May 30, 1899. The nineteenth century was drawing to a close.

The Smithsonian answered Wilbur by sending him a packet of information. This included reports written by a man who would influence the brothers for some time. His name was Octave Chanute. He had written a book entitled *Progress in Flying Machines.* This made him one of the world's most respected men when it came to the subject of flight. He was also from Chicago, which seemed within the Wright brothers' reach.

The bicycle business, the century, and the interests of the Wright brothers all seemed to be moving toward a time of great change.

4

"Flight Is Possible"

The idea that people could fly was hardly new. Throughout history people had watched birds and wished that they, too, could fly. Greek myths had been written about flying. The brilliant Italian Leonardo da Vinci drew sketches of man in flight around A.D. 1500. Some people thought the idea of flying was evil and that only witches did such a thing. Others had jumped from high places to their death in an effort to fly.

Shortly after Milton and Susan Wright had married, the American Civil War broke out, and hot-air balloons were used to spy on enemy troops. Toy helicopters were a plaything that children, including the Wright children, had enjoyed for many years. Also, Asians had been sailing kites for centuries. But controlled, sustained flight still did not exist. Think about the times and the fact that people had no models they could follow. Today when flight is mentioned, everyone can picture the airplane. It has two long wings opposite each other about midway along the body. Two smaller wings come out from the tail. A rudder sticks straight up from the tail. But the people who wanted to fly during the 1890s had no such picture to guide them. All they knew was that birds had wings. Yet no one fully understood what it was that allowed birds to fly.

Many people around the world were now studying the idea of human flight. They tended to be well educated and wealthy enough to afford such a hobby. One of these men was Octave Chanute, a French-born civil engineer who had moved to the United States. During the 1840s Chanute became fascinated with the idea of flight. He read the works of other men and their theories about human flight. But Octave had to work for a living, and he had very little time to devote to his own theories. He therefore took his notes and books and tied them up with a ribbon until he had the time and money he needed to continue his study.

By 1889, the year Susan Wright died, Otto Lilienthal had begun to experiment with flight. He made a major decision to try to fly without using power. This meant gliding. He built at least eighteen gliders of different shapes and sizes—making more than two thousand glides with them. He realized that he needed a dune or hill that would allow him to sail down into a steady wind that came up toward him. This gave him the lift needed to leave the ground. He could then glide as far as the wind would carry him. Lilienthal used his many gliders to calculate how the size and shape of the wing and the strength of the wind affected flight. He then recorded his calculations in a *Table of Normal and Tangential Pressures* (*tangential* means "on a curved surface"). It was the first study of its kind.

Lilienthal loved to fly where others could see him, at times staying aloft long enough to talk to his witnesses. He was a darling of the press, which reported his experiments worldwide. But he wasn't dabbling with flying just for the fun of it. He went up into the air knowing that he might not come down alive. He therefore studied his flight experiments very carefully. He experimented with the shape of wings and finally decided to try curved wings instead of the flat ones that had always been used by other flyers. Curved wings were bowed, or curved—just the way your hand looks when you curve it into the shape of a cup. A curved wing might hold more wind than a flat wing would. His gliders were primitive forms of hang gliders, and he controlled the direction in which he flew by shifting from side to side and swinging his legs. Lilienthal also wrote an important book in 1889, *Bird Flight as the Basis for the Art of Flight.*

Lilienthal's experiments ended in 1896 with the fatal accident Wilbur may have read about to Orville when he was so sick. Lilienthal had recorded flights that lasted for as long as fifteen seconds. That same year, the first successful experiments with flight in the United States were being conducted in secret. This work was being done by Samuel Langley, the scientist at the Smithsonian Institution to which Wilbur was to write his letter in 1899.

Langley was a leading scientist, so his reputation was important to him. He had to be careful not to harm his reputation during his experiments with flight. His fame had been achieved through his studies of the sun and sunspots. This allowed him to become head of the Smithsonian Institution in 1887. By 1891 he had publicly stated his belief that machine-powered flight was possible, based on his studies of surfaces moving through the air. In

May 1896 he flew a thirty-pound model plane with two sets of wings, one set behind the other, several times. One of the flights lasted ninety seconds. It was the world's first sustained flight of a machine that was heavier than air. But, like the model helicopters the Wright boys used to make, would a larger machine be able to stay in the air?

In 1898 Langley received $50,000 from the War Department to increase the size of his flying machine. War with Spain was about to break out, and the military realized the value of a flying machine for spying in time of war. It was the following year, 1899, that the Smithsonian received a letter from an unknown bicycle maker in Ohio. A series of pamphlets the Smithsonian had on issues involving flight were sent in reply, along with a list of recommended books. Wilbur was very pleased to get this information.

In the meantime, Octave Chanute, by now an older man of some wealth, had untied his notes. It was the same year that Lilienthal launched his first glider. Now that he had the time and money he needed, Chanute could pursue his dream of flying. His book, *Progress in Flying Machines*, had been published in 1894. It was on the list of books the Smithsonian had recommended to Wilbur. Chanute lived in Chicago, Illinois, which was more than two hundred miles from Dayton. He was active in a small group of would-be flyers in the 1890s. Chanute believed that mechanical power should be added only after a stable means of flight had been designed. He therefore concentrated his efforts on improving the design of the glider.

On the shores of Lake Michigan just outside of Chicago, Chanute and the men he had hired tried a series of designs beginning in 1896. They chose the lakeshore for its combination of steady wind off the lake and sloping hills. They experimented with many types of gliders that summer. One had as many as twelve wings. The most successful glider, however, had only three pairs of wings, one of which broke off during flight. Yet it was this biplane hang glider that eventually flew 253 feet into the air and stayed there longer than ten seconds. The success of this flight made Octave Chanute one of the world's leading authorities of flying during the 1890s. But by now he had already invested close to $10,000 of his own money and still hadn't beaten Lilienthal's fifteen-second flights. Discouraged, Chanute decided to stop experimenting, but his interest in flight continued.

There were many others who tried to fly during this time. One man in England built a four-ton flyer with 100-foot wings! The machine barely rose two feet off the ground. In other attempts, flyers were killed. Some flyers claimed to have made flights that lasted nearly a minute, but there were no pictures or reliable witnesses. It was well known that some people would do anything to attract the attention of the press. There were organizations of people interested in flight in many parts of the world.

For the two bicycle makers in Dayton, there was plenty to read and much to think about. They ordered the books the Smithsonian had recommended and pored over the pamphlets. They read and reread every scrap of information they had been sent. Orville explained how he and Wilbur felt at this time:

On reading the different works on the subject we were much impressed with the great number of people who had given thought to it [human flight]—among these some of the greatest minds the world has produced....I may mention Leonardo da Vinci...Alexander Graham Bell, inventor of the telephone...Otto Lilienthal...Thomas A. Edison; and Dr. S. P. Langley, secretary and head of the Smithsonian Institution.... But the subject had been brought into disrepute by a number of men of lesser ability...until finally the public was led to believe that flying was...impossible. ...In fact scientists...and mathematicians, had attempted to prove that it would be impossible to build a flying machine that would carry a man.

The brothers quickly cast aside the idea of lighter-than-air flight. They studied both gliding flight and powered flight. They were amazed to discover how little experimentation had been done with steering. To them the ability to control the flight was the key to staying in the air. Within a month after they had begun to read about flying machines, the brothers decided to build one of their own. Orville explained: "After reading the pamphlets sent us by the Smithsonian we became highly enthusiastic with the idea of gliding as sport." They didn't have vast amounts of money to pour into the experiments, so they started with kites. Their first kite was made of shellacked cloth stretched over wings that moved back and forth to control the up-and-down movement.

Many people believed the Wright brothers learned the secret of flight by watching birds. However, Orville explained: "Learning the secret of flight from a bird was a good deal like learning the secret of a magic trick from a magician. After you know the trick and what to look for, you see things you did not notice when you did not know exactly what to look for." The brothers soon realized the importance of being able to move the wings of their machine up and down during flight. They knew *what to do, but not how to do it.* Orville explained: "By this method we thought it would be possible to get greater lift on one side than on the other.... However, we did not see any method of building this device."

It was Wilbur who solved the problem. One evening, as he talked with a customer in 1899, in the bicycle store, he held a light cardboard box in his hand. As Wilbur talked, he found himself moving the box back and forth, twisting it gently. Only to a mind like Wilbur's would this have any meaning. How could a light, flimsy box hold up under that movement? he wondered. If a box did, could the wings of a flying machine? He couldn't wait to tell Orville, who later wrote:

> [O]ne evening... Wilbur showed me a method of getting the same results as we had contemplated in our first idea without the structural defects of the original. He demonstrated... [on] a small pasteboard box which had... the opposite ends removed. By... pressing the corners together, the upper and lower surface of the box were given a... [spiral] twist, presenting the top and bottom surfaces of the box at different angles on the right and left side.

Birds in flight steer by moving their wings at different angles. For a machine to fly, the wings needed to twist, or warp, in flight. The brothers began building a model almost immediately. This kite was more of a model of the glider they wanted to build. It had a wingspan of five feet and was only a foot or so long. Orville later looked back on the day he and Wilbur tried it: "The model was built and, as I remember it, was tested in the latter part of July, 1899. I was not myself present." This wing twisting is called wing warping, and it was a basic key to flight. But Will and Orv weren't convinced yet.

The next step for the brothers was constructing a glider that could carry a person. As they studied the works of other flyers, they thought about the wind they would need for takeoff. With no power source on the glider, only a strong, steady updraft could give them lift. They calculated that they would need a steady wind of fifteen or sixteen miles an hour to take off. This was a more powerful wind than was common in or near Dayton. Thinking about Chanute's work in Chicago, Wilbur wrote to the U.S. Weather Bureau: "We have been doing some experimenting with kites, with a view of constructing one capable of sustaining a man. We expect to carry the experiment further next year. In meantime we wish to obtain if possible a report of the wind [speeds] in Chicago." In reply he received a wind-speed report from weather stations around the country.

Wilbur's next letter was sent to Octave Chanute. He was afraid he wouldn't be taken seriously by someone who was such an authority on flight. But the tone of the letter made its point:

For some years I have been afflicted with the belief that flight is possible to man. My disease has increased ...and I feel it will soon cost me an increased amount of money if not my life. [I plan to] devote my entire time for a few months to experiment in this field.

Assuming that Lilienthal was correct in his ideas ...I conceive that his failure was due chiefly to the inadequacy of his method and of his apparatus....

My business requires that my experimental work

be confined to the months between September and January and I would be particularly thankful for advice...where I could depend on winds of 15 miles per hour without rain....I am certain such localities are rare.

Octave Chanute's reply indicates that he was impressed with Wilbur's letter. He suggested that Wilbur go down a hill with soft sand, as this would be a safe way to experiment. He also said he didn't think a local area would be useful. He recommended San Diego, California, and a part of Florida for steady wind. But Wilbur found that the coasts of South Carolina or Georgia had better sand hills from which to fly. Wilbur promised to think about Chanute's suggestions when he wrote back to thank the world-famous man for his advice. He promised to consider Chanute's suggestions carefully while making his plans. Wilbur's letter ended with a thank-you to Chanute for his offer to meet with him personally. Because the letters were always written by Wilbur, Chanute may not have realized that there were two brothers at work.

The practical Wilbur studied Chanute's suggestions. Because their money was limited, California and Florida were too far away. Then there was the problem of sand hills from which to glide. Orv and Will went back to the *Monthly Weather Reviews* they had gotten from the weather bureau. These would provide them with national information. They wanted to use Chanute's suggestions for sand hills, but they needed to know the strength of the wind in various places. The brothers soon found that the weather service station at Kitty Hawk, North Carolina, reported winds that would meet their needs. It was also closer than anywhere Chanute had suggested. Why did two bicycle makers think they knew more than a world-famous man like Chanute? Orville later explained their thinking:

> From the tables of Lilienthal [whose work they used] we calculated that a machine having an area of a little over 150 square feet would support a man when flown in a wind of sixteen miles an hour. We expected to fly the machine as a kite and in this way we thought it would stay in the air for hours at a time.

Hours at a time—when the greatest minds of the day were getting only *seconds*! This was incredible, but so was the idea of flight itself.

The quiet of the Wright home was an ideal place for the serious planning the brothers now had to do. They had to build a kite and then get it to North Carolina. Kitty Hawk was located on one of the barren islands off the coast of North Carolina just seaward of where the "Lost Colony" of Roanoke of the late 1580s is thought to have been. At the turn of the twentieth century, only fishermen and lighthouses dotted these barrier islands. Orville and Wilbur had read enough about the Cape Hatteras area around Kitty Hawk to know that it was called the "graveyard of the Atlantic." The nickname came from the shifting sands under the sea, from the sudden storms that came during the late fall months, and from the resulting shipwrecks. This was wonderful! Late fall was when they would be able to devote all their time to flying. Would their dream of flying actually come true?

5

"A Vacation of Several Weeks"

Orville and Wilbur had settled on the Outer Banks along the Atlantic Ocean as the best place to try out their glider. This thin band of islands lies like a shoestring just off the coast of North Carolina. The line of islands runs from Virginia to southern North Carolina along the zigzag coast, bending at Cape Hatteras. It ends more than 200 miles later near the port of Wilmington. Because these small islands jut out into the Atlantic, winds from the ocean usually blow over them.

During the summer of 1900, the Outer Banks were a warm and pleasant place to be. But they were hard to reach because there were no roads connecting the mainland to the islands. This was why there were few homes and only a small population of fishers along much of these barrier islands. One of the few people who lived there was William Tate, the postmaster of Kitty Hawk. Wilbur had written to the weather bureau station at Kitty Hawk to learn more about the area's weather during the months when he and Orville would be free to pursue what they regarded as their hobby. Bill, as Tate was called, learned of Wilbur's interest and sent a more detailed response than did the weather bureau. In a small, sleepy fishing village, the news of these men who wanted to fly had created quite a stir.

Bill's letter had made the Outer Banks sound ideal— sloping sand dunes, steady winds with gusts that were just the right strength, and friendly people who would be glad to be of service. But, Bill warned, by November the weather would turn stormy and unpredictable, so the Wrights needed to get to the islands early in the fall. Orville and Wilbur therefore got to work in August, building their first glider. They wrote to Octave Chanute for advice on the type of materials they should use, and his reply came quickly. Even though the brothers managed to make al- most everything they needed, the glider still ended up costing $15 to build. They would get the final parts, the spruce spars that would shape the wings, closer to Kitty Hawk. Spars were wooden poles on which the wing cloth was stretched. Moving a large glider, even in pieces, wouldn't be an easy job.

The brothers were discovering that getting themselves to Kitty Hawk wouldn't be easy either. Kitty Hawk was nearly 600 miles southeast of Dayton. So much planning had gone into the glider that the brothers hadn't taken much time to plan the trip itself. Katharine wrote to her father on September 5: "We are in an uproar getting Will off. The trip will do him good. I don't think he will be reckless. If they can arrange it, Orv will go down as soon as

Will gets the machine ready." The thinking was that Wilbur would go ahead, find the spruce for the spars, arrange housing, and assemble "the machine." In the meantime, Orivlle would get the bicycle business ready to be left for several weeks.

The first leg of the journey was easy enough. A train ran from Dayton to Norfolk, Virginia, which was a distance of less than fifty miles north of Kitty Hawk. Both were on the Atlantic, and all Wilbur had to do was get the spruce for the spars and go south to Kitty Hawk. But it took twenty-four bumpy hours on a noisy train just to get to Norfolk. Wilbur wearily got off the train, glad to be so close to his goal. He spent the night, then went to look for the eighteen-foot spruce strips he would need to make the spars. But there were none to be found in Norfolk. Disappointed, Wilbur had to settle for sixteen-foot lengths of white pine instead. The pine wouldn't be as strong as the spruce, and the glider was designed for eighteen-foot spars. This meant that changes would have to be made. The $7.70 Wilbur had to pay for the pine seemed high, and the glider now had $22.70 invested in it.

Wilbur then began looking for transportation to Kitty Hawk, which seemed simple enough. With a cruel heat wave pushing the temperature close to 100 degrees, he got to Elizabeth City south of Norfolk. Here he expected to take a ferry to Kitty Hawk. As Wilbur explained it:

I spent several days waiting for the boat to Kitty Hawk. No one seems to know anything about the place or how to get there. At last on Tuesday [September 11, 1900] left. I engaged passage with Israel Perry on his flat-bottom schooner fishing boat.

The passage was an adventurous one. The boat was leaky, dirty, and its sides barely rose out of the water. The trip took longer than Wilbur had expected, including a night spent bailing water to keep the boat from sinking. When they finally arrived at Kitty Hawk, the sun had already set, and the fishermen had turned in for the night. Another night on the boat was passed in the company of the huge mosquitoes for which the Outer Banks were famous.

The next morning, a full week after leaving Dayton, Wilbur made his way to the home of Bill Tate. There he was greeted as warmly as Bill had said he would be. A hearty breakfast quickly appeared, and the exhausted Wilbur decided that his luck had finally changed. Across the table sat a smiling Bill, who would be a close and useful friend in the time ahead. Wilbur described Tate and his home in a letter he wrote to his father on September 23:

His occupation is fishing in the fishing season, which begins about Oct. 1st and lasts for about three months. His house is a two-story frame with unplaned siding, not painted, no plaster on the walls, which are sealed with pine not varnished. He has no carpets at all, very little furniture, no books or pictures.

While Wilbur was writing this letter, Orville was getting ready to join him at Kitty Hawk. He had left the bicycle business with an employee, Harry Dillion. He had an uneasy feeling about Dillion, but finding someone to do this temporarily wasn't easy. Since Wilbur had briefed him on all the problems he'd had reaching Kitty Hawk, Orville was able to make the trip in four days. Even that was exhausting, though. He had to bring a tent with him because there was no hotel at Kitty Hawk. Their home would be a campsite while they stayed at Kitty Hawk.

As Orville journeyed toward his brother, Wilbur wrote to his father explaining his progress and his plans:

I have my machine nearly finished. It is not to have a motor and is not expected to fly in any true sense of the word. My idea is merely to experiment and practice with a view of solving the problem of equilibrium. I have plans which I hope to find much in advance of the methods tried by previous experimenters. When once a machine is in proper control under all conditions, the motor problem will be quickly solved.

Sounding like a son who didn't want to worry his father, Wilbur continued:

In my experiments I do not expect to rise many feet above the ground, and in case I am upset there is nothing but soft sand to strike on. I do not intend to take dangerous chances, both because I have no wish to get hurt and because a fall would stop my experimenting, which I would not like at all.

By the first week in October, "the machine" was finished. It was quite different from the gliders Chanute had built. The brothers didn't want the tail to dig into the sand, pulling the glider down as it struggled to take off. So they moved the rudder in front of the double-decker wings with their sixteen-foot spars. This would allow them to land safely, and the glider could still be steered—up and down—by the front rudder. Also, the pilot would be lying flat along the lower wing, rather than sitting with his feet hanging down, to help catch the glider as it settled back to earth. Thanks to the soft sands of Kitty Hawk, the glider could coast without being damaged. The wings had been covered with soft cloth and placed one over the other. No one in Kitty Hawk had ever seen such a thing.

Sometime during that first week of October, the brothers and their new friend Bill Tate took the glider out for a test. The weather bureau records showed wind gusts of twenty-five to thirty miles an hour—enough to fly in. There were no records of this first flight; not keeping such records seems unlike the Wright brothers. It is known that the first flights were manned so they could test the glider's ability to soar while someone controlled it. On October 14 Orville wrote to Katharine:

> We have been having a fine time. Altogether we have had the machine out three different days, of from two to four hours each time. Monday night and all day Tuesday we had a terrific wind, blowing 36 miles an hour. Wednesday morning the Kitty Hawkers were out early peering around the edge of the woods and out of their upstairs windows to see whether our camp was still in existence. We were all right, however, and though the wind continued up to 30 miles, got the machine out to give it another trial.

In that heavy wind they flew the machine as a glider. When it was about twenty feet high, they worked the rudder's controls to keep it from continuing to rise, which it would have done. They used what Orville called a "ducking string" to bring the glider back down as they practiced steering it.

At one point that afternoon, as Wilbur and Orville worked on some minor adjustments on the grounded machine, a sudden burst of wind caught one wing and lifted it up. The glider was thrown about twenty feet away. Seeing the wrecked glider, the brothers nearly gave up and returned to Dayton. But the Wrights weren't quitters. It took three days to repair the glider as October wore on. Given Bill's warning about the weather in November, there was little time to lose. The fierce fall storms called nor'easters were beginning and often hit at night. The campers then had to cope with darkness, along with winds as strong as 45 miles an hour. On top of this, they had to hold down a flapping tent and a machine that had been made to fly in winds that were only blowing twenty to twenty-five miles an hour. Orville wrote to Katharine about the nor'easters:

We have just passed through one which took up two or three wagonloads of sand from the N.E. end of our tent and piled it up eight inches deep on the flying machine, which we had anchored about fifty feet southwest. The wind shaking the roof and sides of the tent sounds exactly like thunder. When we crawl out of the tent to fix things the sand fairly blinds us. It blows across the ground in clouds. We certainly can't complain of the place. We came down here for wind and sand, and we have got them.

In the few days they had left, Wilbur and Orville tried unmanned tests in light winds. The machine flew steadily. This first glider was a large kitelike object with two wings, one stacked on top of the other, with a wing surface of 165 square feet. It was controlled two ways: first, the up-or-down movement of the nose was controlled by an elevator, which made the machine nose up to lift or down to lower itself. Second, the side-to-side movement was controlled by wing warping, which allowed the wings' tips to flex opposite each other, giving the ability to steer the machine left and right.

Things weren't going as well at home, though. Katharine had written to say that she had had to dismiss the young man Orville had hired. This meant the shop was closed. The likelihood of serious storms was growing, so it was time to think about going home.

The brothers had enjoyed the rugged setting and the people of Kitty Hawk. They had to do much of their own hunting and fishing, and they were treated as celebrities wherever they went. As always, they simply divided the chores between them. Orville did most of the cooking, and Wilbur did the dishwashing. There wasn't much to do in Kitty Hawk, but the brothers never grew tired of studying the soaring shorebirds and how they flew. They were also moved by the remote beauty of Kitty Hawk. In a letter to Katharine, Orville wrote:

> The sunsets here are the prettiest I have ever seen. The clouds light up in all colors in the background, with deep blue clouds of various shapes fringed with gold before. The moon rises in much the same style, and lights up this pile of sand almost like day. I read my watch at all hours of the night on moonless nights without the aid of any other light than that of the stars shining on the canvas of the tent.

Katharine wasn't there to see these things for herself, but Orville would make it come alive for her. The brothers always managed to do this. For her part, Katharine had always had a lively interest in the activities of these two of her brothers. A young woman in her twenties, she had graduated from Oberlin College and now taught at Steele High School in Dayton. Like her brothers, however, she was not married and still lived at home.

The records of exactly what happened during this first fall in Kitty Hawk are incomplete. However, it is known that the brothers experimented with manned glides and about a dozen other flights during this time. In all, they probably had only about two full minutes of manned gliding. The longest glides probably lasted no more than fifteen to twenty seconds and did not go beyond 400 feet. But the machine flew, and the experience, along with their notebook full of observations, would keep the brothers busy during that winter in Dayton. The glider itself was not saved for history. It was given, full of cracks and mended tears, to Bill Tate as the brothers headed home. It was too cumbersome to dismantle and lug back to Dayton. Bill was glad to have the material, which his wife made into clothes for their daughters. The wood, too, came in handy. It was always hard to find on the windswept shores of the Outer Banks.

On November 16, 1900, Wilbur wrote to Octave Chanute:

> In October my brother and myself spent a vacation of several week at Kitty Hawk, North Carolina, experimenting with a soaring machine....It is an ideal place for gliding experiments....The person who goes there must take everything he will possibly need, for he cannot depend on getting any needed article from the outside world in less than three weeks.

He then went into the details of the design of the flyer and the things he and Orville had learned from it. Although

Wilbur was clearly pleased about what they had done, his letter indicated that there was more to be learned. The brothers spent that winter of 1900–1901 studying the tables developed by Otto Lilienthal. They also exchanged letters with Octave Chanute and wrote two articles about their experiments. They then waited for the next fall, when they could again take a flyer back to the blustery winds of Kitty Hawk.

6

The "Wind Straightener"

The winter of 1900–1901 was a very important one for the Wright brothers. They weren't completely satisfied with the glider they had made during the summer; a new one had to be built. They would use the winter months when business was slow to design a new and bigger glider. What they wanted to build was somewhat like a kite that could carry a man on board. They knew that a bigger wing meant more surface area. The greater the surface area, the more lift they could expect. Again, they went to Lilienthal's tables and added more curve to the wing. They would again build the glider in Dayton and take it to Kitty Hawk.

The glider they built this time was huge by the standards of the day. It had seven-foot-wide wings that extended twenty-two feet. It weighed a staggering 98 pounds! Adding a 140-pound pilot to the glider would increase its weight to more than 240 pounds. When Octave Chanute heard about it, he warned the brothers against flying in such a huge machine. But they already knew more about flight than their friend did. What Chanute didn't know, however, time would prove to him.

The brothers were so excited about trying out their new glider that they were willing to leave their bicycle business in July to get to North Carolina early. They had recently hired a pleasant older man named Charlie Taylor, who seemed like one of the family. He called Orville and Wilbur "the boys," while they called him "Pop." They trusted Pop to run the business while they took another "vacation" at Kitty Hawk.

The two brothers left for the coast of North Carolina in early July 1901 and were greeted by a storm that cost them time getting to Kitty Hawk. In a letter to Octave Chanute, Wilbur explained: "We reached Kitty Hawk several days later than expected owing to the greatest storm in history of the place." There were winds as strong as eighty-three miles per hour, and it rained for a full week. These weren't the best conditions for their plans, but the brothers went ahead anyway. They left Kitty Hawk for the area called Kill Devil Hills, which was actually a few miles south of Kitty Hawk and faced the Atlantic Ocean. Here the winds could come straight off the ocean. Because it was a fishing village, Kitty Hawk faced the sound—an area of calmer waters between the barrier islands and the North Carolina coast.

Orville and Wilbur had done some flying on Kill Devil Hills the year before. There were three hills there, the tallest of which was about a hundred feet high. Because the winter storms reshaped the area each year, its exact height actually changed from one year to the next. They were able to build a sixteen- by twenty-five foot shed at Kill Devil Hills so that the glider would be protected from summer storms. But what they really needed was protection from the huge crop of hungry mosquitoes that were everywhere. They used mosquito netting at night, but it almost seemed as if the giant bugs would carry them off when they swarmed. This wasn't the type of flight the brothers wanted!

Perhaps the reason that people think of Kitty Hawk and not Kill Devil Hills when they think about the Wright brothers comes from the fact that the nearest village with a post office was in Kitty Hawk and the brothers' letters are, therefore, addressed that way. Among other letters they wrote was one to Octave Chanute, who continued to offer them encouragement and support. He also wanted to send them some help. He offered them two people. The first person was E. C. Huffaker, who had built gliders for Chanute. Orville and Wilbur disliked Huffaker almost immediately. The second person Chanute sent was George A. Spratt, who would become an instant friend to the brothers. Chanute sent Spratt because he had some training in medicine. Chanute always worried that these two young bicycle makers would have a terrible accident. Besides, Spratt, too, had a keen interest in flying. Chanute paid the men's travel costs, and the Wright brothers provided them with food and shelter. The mosquitoes must have loved having two more people to feast on!

The new glider was ready for its first test by July 27, 1901. It flew farther than the earlier glider did, but it wasn't as level in flight. The brothers set a personal record of 315 feet. They had stayed aloft, or in the air, for nineteen seconds. The landings were soft because of a rudder they had built on the front of the glider. But it was hard to move, and the big glider didn't pick up speed as they had expected it would. Something had to be changed. Was the problem one of bigger being less steady, as it had been with the toy helicopter?

On July 30 Wilbur wrote this entry in his diary:

> The lift is not much over one third that indicated by the Lilienthal tables.... [W]e find that our hopes of obtaining actual practice in the air are decreased to about one fifth what we hoped....
>
> The good points as indicated by the experiments already made are these:....
>
> 1. The machine is strong....
> 2. With less than an hour's practice we succeeded in getting a free flight of over 300 feet....
> 3. We have experimented safely with a machine of over 300 square feet surface in winds as high as 18 miles per hour. Previous experimenters had pronounced a machine of such size impracticable to construct and impossible to manage....
> 4. The lateral [sideways] balance of the machine seems all that could be desired....

But there were problems to overcome. As Orville later explained, "As a result of these experiments we soon decided to reduce the curvature of the wings." If that worked, then Lilienthal's tables had to be wrong.

It is at this point that the real genius of the Wright brothers begins to show itself. The Lilienthal tables had never been questioned by anyone else. But the brothers learned first by doing, then applying the science of it later. They used a "system of posts and wires about midway

Orville and Wilbur Wright hold their 1901 glider as it is photographed near Kitty Hawk, North Carolina.

between the front and rear spars," as Orville explained it. The Wrights were able to look at a problem and give it a practical solution. They had passed from learning based on other people's work to inventing their own flying machine using the principles they themselves had observed. The experiments they made proved that they were right. They experimented with the wings to see how the angle of the wing and the speed of wind affected the lifting power of the wings. They found that it was only about one-third of what Lilienthal's tables on air pressure had estimated that it would be. The brothers had come a long way—from the idea of wing warping that occurred to Wilbur when he flexed the cardboard box that evening in

One of the Wright brothers on the 1901 glider near Kitty Hawk, North Carolina.

the bicycle shop to proving that Otto Lilienthal had been wrong! But the problem of controlled flight was far from solved.

The Wright brothers used the summer of 1901 to launch many experimental flights. Orville reported: "Several hundred flights were made. I do not know the exact number. The flights ranged all the way from fifty feet to nearly four hundred feet in length. Quite a number were made of a distance of three hundred feet or more." During these experiments they found that wind coming from the side caused the machine to lift too much. By drooping the wing tips and experimenting with the curvature of the wing, they improved this. However, the problem of drift—slipping sideways in the air—continued.

66

In the meantime, Octave Chanute became so interested in the brothers' experiments that he came to Kill
Devil Hills in August. He noticed that several flights lasted
longer than fifteen seconds and went farther than 300 feet.
But things came to a standstill when the wings got stuck in
the sand during one flight and several parts were broken.
Poor Wilbur, who was on board at the time, was thrown
into the rudder. He must have been glad that George
Spratt was there to check his bruises!

By August 22, 1901, it was time to go home to Dayton.
Chanute, Huffaker, and Spratt had left by then, and Kitty
Hawk was preparing for the fall fishing season. Even Bill
Tate wasn't available. Orville summed things up in this
way:

> Our experiments of 1901 were rather discouraging to
> us because we felt that they had demonstrated that
> some of the most firmly established laws...were
> mostly, if not entirely, incorrect. At first we had taken
> up the problem merely as a matter of sport, but now it
> was apparent that if we were to make much progress it
> would be necessary to get better tables from which to
> make our calculations.

The "discouragement" that Orville mentions gives some
insight into the way the brothers approached any problem
they were having. Imagine being the people who would
solve the mystery of flight, being high school dropouts
who had proved that the most respected theories of flying
were wrong, and being "discouraged." They viewed their
problems as something to be solved, not as a reason for
giving up. The first year they had logged, or achieved,
about two full minutes of flying. Now, in 1901, they had
made several hundred flights on a machine that most

experts said wouldn't fly! Based on how much they had learned the first year, the Wright brothers had much more to learn during the winter of 1901–02.

The brothers continued to make a strong impression on Octave Chanute. In fact, he now wanted Wilbur to address the Western Society of Engineers in Chicago. Why did he ask Wilbur and not Orville? The answer is that it was Wilbur who had written most of the letters. He was also the older brother. Besides, Wilbur was the more serious of the brothers. Orville was more the fun lover who played pranks and was willing to put things off. As Katharine explained to her father, who was away on one of his business trips for the church:

> Through Mr. Chanute, Will has an invitation to make a speech before the Western Society of Engineers, which has a meeting in Chicago in a couple of weeks. ...His subject is his Gliding Experiments....I nagged him into going....We don't hear anything but flying machine and engine from morning till night. I'll be glad when school begins so I can escape.

The family was worried about what Wilbur would say and how he would look. After all, it was Orville who was the dandy and always dressed well. Wilbur almost lived in another world, consumed by the idea of flight. Katharine explained this in a letter to her father: "Orville offered all his clothes so off went 'Ullam,' arrayed in Orv's shirt, collars, cuffs, cuff-links, and overcoat. We discovered that to some extent 'clothes do make the man' for you never saw Will look so 'swell.' "

Wilbur's speech was well received, and it led to a greater awareness of the Wright brothers and their work.

Later that winter he would write an article entitled "Some Aeronautical Experiments." (The word *aeronautical* comes from two Greek words: *aero*, meaning "of the air" or "aircraft," and *nautical*, meaning "seaman" or "navigating a ship.") Chanute had copies of the journal article sent to many other, more widely read magazines. The article was reprinted in *Scientific American* and British magazines, among others. While Wilbur was in Chicago, Orville was left at home, worried about both his clothes and the person who was wearing them! Were the Lilienthal tables correct, after all? Would Will be laughed at? How could they accomplish more in their experiments next summer?

This last question was one that Orville could work on. Taking an old starch box, he built a small wind tunnel. The Wright brothers didn't invent the wind tunnel, but they did put it to an important use. A wind tunnel is, literally, a human-made tunnel into which wind is forced to test the effect of air pressure on models. This is also done with models of airplane wings to test the effect of wind pressure on them. In a wind tunnel many designs and angles of wings could be tested while the brothers waited to get back to Kitty Hawk. The "wind" came from a small fan driven by a motor they built.

Although his speech was a success, when Wilbur returned from Chicago he wrote to Chanute: "At least two thirds of my time in the past six months has been devoted to aeronautical matters. Unless I decide to devote myself to something else than a business career, I must give closer attention to my regular work for a while." Chanute understood and wrote back: "If your method and machine are reliable you have done a great work, and have advanced knowledge greatly.... I very much regret, in the interest of Science, that you have reached a stopping place ... for I see as yet no money return for the pursuit, save from possible exhibition." About a month later, however, Wilbur was writing to Chanute about the larger "pressure testing machine" he and Orville had built. In it they would test wings of more than 200 shapes and designs in hopes of making the 1902 flyer better than any they had built so far. One design should have produced maximum lift at five degrees, but the wind tunnel showed that an angle of eighteen degrees was best. The shape and design of the wing was important for providing the glider with maximum lift.

Wilbur called the tunnel a "wind straightener." This was different from what he called "natural wind," which is what was found at Kitty Hawk. In the wind straightener, the brothers could experiment with maximum lift and wind speed, but the results would be useful only if they worked outdoors in natural wind. The brothers learned a lot from these experiments. They now understood that in order to fly, their machine had to work in an ocean of air. The air would be forced below the wings to lift the flyer against gravity. The reason for gliding downhill was to use speed in this ocean of air. Once the flyer was airborne, control became a concern because the craft could go out of control in any direction. The Wright brothers were the first to prove that stacked wings, which Chanute preferred, had less lift than single wings.

To help the brothers further, Octave Chanute offered to find a gift of money from a wealthy person who wanted to see people learn to fly. But this offer was turned down because the Wright brothers felt that their work was only an expensive hobby and there was little chance of making any money from it. Of what real use would learning to fly be anyway? There was no time to dwell on this question, however. A church crisis involving Milton Wright forced them to drop everything and give their father the support he needed. A man who worked for the church had been accused of stealing funds, and the members were soon divided between support for Milton Wright and support for this man. Wilbur spent hours going over the church's financial books to prove that his father was right. In the end, he did just that. But the church suffered from the incident, and the family lost a great deal of time and energy.

When the church crisis was over, the brothers went back to their flight plans. That winter they wrote to George Spratt questioning the Lilienthal tables and the work others were doing. They also worked on their own idea that sheet metal should replace the fabric covering they had used on the wings of their glider. They even thought about adding a gasoline engine to give the glider its own power.

This was an exciting time to live in the American Midwest. The St. Louis Exhibition, a huge display of new inventions, was being planned. Prizes for new inventions were offered, and Octave Chanute thought the prize for human flight was worth considering. The newspapers carried many stories about experiments with flight and what others were learning about flying. Samuel Langley, thought to be the world's leading authority on flight, was often written about in Smithsonian publications and in the popular press. Many reporters, however, made fun of the idea of flight because it was so clear that it simply couldn't be done. They felt that if men like Langley couldn't make this happen, no one could.

By the summer of 1902, the Wright brothers had begun to look forward to another "vacation" at Kitty

Hawk. Early in July, Chanute visited them in Dayton to see what progress they had made. Again he offered money, and once more it was turned down. He then offered to have some experts join the brothers on the North Carolina coast. These experts would try out Chanute's latest designs and help the young bicycle makers with theirs. Except for George Spratt, the brothers preferred to work alone. But how could they turn down their generous supporter? They would be joined by William Avery, a Chicago engineer who built Chanute's gliders. Augustus M. Herring, who did his own experiments with flyers, would also be with them, but he would prove to be a real troublemaker.

By August, Katharine's support for her brothers' flying experiments could be seen in a letter she wrote to her father:

> The flying machine is in process of making now. Will spins the sewing machine around by the hour while Orv. squats around making places to sew.... Will is thin and nervous and so is Orv. They will be all right when they get down in the sand where the salt breezes blow, etc.... They think that life at Kitty Hawk cures all ills you know.

The new, improved 1902 glider was very different from the others. Each one was more advanced than the one before it. The 1900 flyer looked more like a kite than an airplane. The bigger 1901 flyer was more solid and complex. But the 1902 flyer shows how much the brothers had learned from their flights of the past two years and from the "wind straightening machine" the winter before. The wings were now thirty-two feet long and had a larger lifting area. They were also now six times longer than their width, and the frame was stronger. In addition, a tail had been added to increase control in the air. The Wright brothers had always thought that the biggest problem of flight was achieving stability once the flyer was in the air. This new machine showed the work they had done in this area.

As the summer of 1902 faded, the brothers again headed for Kitty Hawk. This time they reached Elizabeth City in only thirty-three hours. There they learned that the schooner the *Lou Willis* would be setting sail for Kitty Hawk. They would have to move quickly! But there would be time to get gasoline and a stove before they set sail. Life at Kitty Hawk got better each summer.

The trip to Kitty Hawk took longer than was expected, but the brothers arrived safely. After finding their building at Kill Devil Hills, they dug a well, added a loft, repaired winter damage, and worked on being more comfortable. Wilbur wrote Katharine:

> We drove our well a few days ago by a method we shall probably patent...and obtained water...[which] is the best in Kitty Hawk....So far, in addition to cookery, etc., we have exercised ourselves in the trades of carpentering, furniture making, upholstering, well driving, and will add house moving next week.

Wilbur and Orville were masters of anything and everything mechanical. They even built and used a sand bicycle to speed their trips to check for mail at the post office in Kitty Hawk. The patent Wilbur mentioned is a means of protecting a new idea or design from being stolen by someone else. A patent is a government document giving the inventor or owner of the patent rights to the invention for a certain number of years. The owner of a patent has the exclusive, or only, right to make and sell what is patented.

Once the camp at Kill Devil Hills had been fixed up, the brothers began to put the flyer together. By September 19, 1902, it was ready, but the experiments were delayed until September 22. Bill Tate came to help them experiment with using the flyer as a kite. When hit from the side by a sudden gust of wind, the older flying machines could crash. In a steady wind they experimented to see whether the problem with crosswinds had been solved with the new flyer. It had! The lessons the brothers had learned in the wind straightener paid off!

On September 23 Orville was added to the flyer as its pilot. After a few glides, he lost control of the flyer when one wing flipped up and he moved the controls the wrong way. Suddenly the flyer was at a forty-five-degree angle in the front and falling toward the soft sand. Wilbur and Bill watched in fear. As Orville explained: "The result was a heap of flying machine cloth and sticks, with me in the center without a bruise or scratch." It took several days to fix the flyer.

By now Augustus Herring had arrived on the *Lou Willis* with Chanute's latest multiwing glider. Orville and Wilbur took one look at this glider and decided that it was hopelessly out of date. They were right. By October 11 Herring had given up on it. Chanute himself now came to Kitty Hawk to see how his glider and the work of Orville and Wilbur were doing. The success of the Wrights' glider was obvious. Wilbur wrote to his father:

Our new machine is a very great improvement over anything we had built before and over anything any one has built...a power machine can fly with much

Octave Chanute (seated at the left) visits the Wright brothers' camp at Kill Devil Hill, North Carolina.

less power. The new machine is also much more controllable than any heretofore built so the danger is correspondingly reduced.... Everything is so much more satisfactory that we now believe that the flying problem is really nearing its solution.

The Wright brothers had never seemed to really doubt that they could do what no one else had been able to do. They simply looked at flight as a problem they had to solve.

As October wore on, they became busier. Lorin, their older brother, and George Spratt came to Kitty Hawk to visit. By now Herring and Chanute had left, and Orville wrote to tell Katharine what a good time the four of them were having. He noted that George was "a fine fellow to be with." They spent time exploring the woods as well as working on their flyer. Unlike 1900, when they made only a few flights, they now did a great many. In fact, it was almost becoming routine.

It is not known exactly how many flights the brothers made that October. But a letter Orville wrote to Katharine clearly shows that they got the results they wanted:

> Day before yesterday we had a wind—about 30 miles per hour, and glided in it without any trouble. That was the highest wind a gliding machine had ever been in, so we now hold all the records! The largest machine, the longest time in the air, the smallest angle of descent, and the highest wind!!!

Within just two days, they had made 250 glides ranging from 7 to 16 seconds long. One of these glides went beyond 600 feet. Wind warping provided the side-to-side control the pilot needed when the flyer banked, or turned. Once in a while, however, the flyer would mysteriously turn up and slip sideways until the lower wing tip dragged in the sand. Wilbur and Orville called this "well-digging," and it gave them something to think about when that wonderful summer of 1902 ended.

7

"Success Assured. Keep Quiet"

Orville and Wilbur had learned many things during the hundreds of glides they took in 1902. This gave them much to think about as the winter of 1903 approached. The newspapers of the day were often filled with humorous stories that poked fun at the idea of people trying to fly. The Wright brothers had no desire to become objects of humor or scorn.

This was probably why they became more secretive about their plans. They had no interest in attracting the attention of the press or the public, but their experiments had become well known to Samuel Langley. In November 1902 Wilbur wrote to Octave Chanute: "We received from Mr. Langley, a few days before we finished our experiments at Kitty Hawk [in 1902], . . . a letter, inquiring whether there would be time for him to reach us and witness some of our trials before we left. We replied that it would be scarcely possible." Further on, Wilbur noted: "He made no mention of his experiments on the Potomac." These experiments were often featured in the news. After all, in 1898 the U.S. War Department had given Langley $50,000 to make an airplane the military could use. After a series of failures and limited successes, Langley had finally built an aerodrome (*aero* means "of the air," and *drome* means "running") with an eighty-five-foot launching track. All this was put on a flatboat and taken onto the Potomac River near Washington, D.C., for tests. There were many reporters on hand to see what would happen.

Meanwhile, in December 1902 Octave Chanute received a letter from Samuel Langley. He wanted to know more about the Kitty Hawk experiments. He especially wanted to know how the Wright brothers' glider was controlled. When he told Orville and Wilbur about the letter, Chanute said it "seemed rather cheeky."

Orville and Wilbur had clear plans for that winter. They explained some of these plans in a letter to Chanute:

> It is our intention next year to build a machine much larger and about twice as heavy as our present machine. With it we will work out problems relating to starting and handling heavy-weight machines, and if we find it under satisfactory control in flight, we will proceed to mount a motor.

Wilbur gave more details to his friend George Spratt: "We are thinking of building a machine next year with 500 sq. ft. surface, about 40 ft. × 6 ft. 6 in." A flying machine of this size had been unthinkable even one year earlier. But the brothers clearly saw themselves building a machine that was very different from any they had made so far. As the thousands of letters from them clearly show, they called this one a "flyer" and not just a "machine." Most of the letters are from Will, because as Orv explained: "Will seems to enjoy writing so I leave all the literary part of our work to him." Wilbur's letters often refer to "I" when talking about both himself and Orville. Perhaps that was just his way of thinking about the two of them so closely simply as one team. There are many hundreds of letters between the brothers and their family, mainly to their father and to Katharine. They provide insights into their thoughts and are signed formally. Many of the letters end with "Affectionately, your son, Wilbur" or something like that. Even their loving father signed his letters, "Your father, Milton Wright."

During that important winter of 1902–03, they still thought of family first, although everyone was caught up in the work on their flyer. Milton Wright wrote in his diary in February 1903: "The boys increased the flow of gas by putting a 'snorter' in the radiator in my room. Our gas radiators are of their invention and their making."

A photograph the Wrights took of their bicycle shop in early 1903 shows how much the flyer had taken over their business. The huge wings took up so much space that there was hardly room for customers or their bicycles. But the plans for this flyer involved much more than simply making a bigger, heavier machine.

The new flyer had four major problems to overcome:

1. *Control.* The flyer had to remain stable in the air, and the pilot had to be able to steer it. The Wright brothers placed a rudder—used for moving the flyer from side to side—behind each of the huge wings. They then put a double-wing "elevator" in front of the main wings. This device would control the up-and-down movement of

the flyer. All controls had to be within the pilot's reach.

2. *Size and lift.* As the machine got bigger and heavier, the ratio of wing size to lift became more important. This was also true of the wing warping, which allowed the wing tips to flex independently in flight. The wing tips were flexed, drooping at the tips to control gusts of wind that came from the side. Each pair of wings warped independently at the control of the pilot.

3. *Propellers.* In 1903 no propellers had been used in the air, only the "screws" that moved ships through water. The Wright brothers already knew that they couldn't rely on the work of others, so they invented their own propellers to help their flyer "swim" through the air. When they found out that the screw propellers used in the water would be of no use to them, Orville explained: "When we found that we could not do this, we began to study the screw propeller from an entirely theoretical standpoint, since we saw that with the small capital [money] we possessed we would not be able to develop an efficient air propeller on the 'cut and try' plan." In other words, they would have to develop their own theory about how propellers worked and try it out at Kitty Hawk. They then built two eight-foot-long propellers designed to move in the opposite direction from each other to increase side-to-side stability.

4. *Motor.* In 1900 Wilbur had assured his father: "When once a machine is under proper control under all conditions, the motor problem would be quickly solved." But the brothers couldn't find an engine to meet their needs. As they had done so many times before, they solved this problem by building their own. What they came up with weighed 180 pounds, nearly 50 pounds more than they had expected. This didn't even include the quarter-

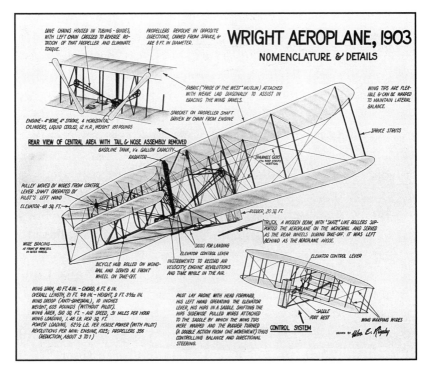

A diagram of the 1903 Wright Flyer.

gallon gas tank. The engine produced twelve horsepower.
If the propellers worked, this would be more than enough
to get them into the air. Having such a heavy engine on the
pilot's left meant that the left wing had to be four inches
longer than the right wing. This would make up for the 50-
pound difference between the pilot and the motor. The
flyer the brothers finally finished weighed in at an incredible 625 pounds with a man on board! As Orv wrote
explaining all this to George Spratt: "P.S. Please do not
mention the fact that we are building a power machine to
anybody. The newspapers would take great delight in
following us in order to record our *troubles*."

Much of what the Wright brothers did that winter was very technical. But all of it showed what geniuses they were. Remember, they had to be especially creative because their money was limited. Also, because this was all so new to the world, many of the materials they needed simply weren't available. They had to invent as they went along—and they had to do it cheaply. For example, they couldn't use tires on a sandy beach, so they designed the "junction railroad," as they called it. The flyer would roll along a single rail that was sixty feet long and made of wooden two-by-fours covered with a thin strip of metal. They would assemble it in Kitty Hawk, and it cost four dollars to make!

While the flyer was being finished and the busy bicycle months of summer rolled on, the Wrights' old friend Octave Chanute went to Europe. He spoke about the Wright brothers' experiments while he was in Paris, and the newspapers there carried stories about them. Not surprisingly, it wasn't too long before the French began experimenting with a flyer like the Wright brothers'. In fact, a Captain Ferdinand Ferber of the French military wanted to buy a Wright flyer. He also wanted to go to Kitty Hawk to see the brothers at work. Except for Chanute, Spratt, and their trusted friends in Kitty Hawk, however, Orville and Wilbur preferred to work alone.

By August of 1903 the Wrights were once again busy packing for the journey to Kitty Hawk. This trip would be a massive undertaking. There were more than 600 pounds of flyer parts, equipment, supplies, and little things they would need to increase the comfort of their campsite on the Outer Banks. It was late in September before they finally set out to fly on the winds of Kitty Hawk.

When they arrived on the Outer Banks, they found

that the previous winter there had been a hard one. A huge storm had knocked their building off its foundation and dragged it two feet away. Sand was piled high, and so was their gear. They had to construct a second building just to house everything. They used good flying days to glide with the 1902 machine, while the new building and the 1903 flyer were put together on days when they couldn't fly. The 1902 machine worked beautifully. Early in October, Orville reported to Katharine: "These two days of gliding have made us much more expert in handling the machine, and the next day we have 18 to 20 miles of wind we expect to go up and stay for at least several minutes."

By now the Wright brothers had begun to feel like expert flyers. A letter to their father reported: "We have increased our time for length of flight to 43 seconds, which is 1 ⅔ over last year's record and about three times the best of anyone else." The weather on Kitty Hawk would be good for only a short time, however. A terrible storm that lasted four days hit the area just after the crates with the flyer parts arrived. The wind blew so hard that it lifted their tar-paper roof and they had to go out into the storm to fix it. Then the water on the island rose so high that part of their building was underwater. All they could do during these trying days was survive. But the storm did pass, and assembly of the flyer began at last.

It wasn't easy to get news on Kitty Hawk, but by mid-October, Wilbur was aware that Samuel Langley was trying to fly his expensive machine. But he failed. On November 1, Orville wrote to Katharine: "I suppose you have read in the papers the account of the failure of Langley's big machine.... They found they had no control of the machine whatever.... We have been in the air hundreds and hundreds of times, and have pretty well worked out the problem of control." By the time this letter was written, the 1902 glider had risen as much as sixty feet off the ground and had stayed up for more than one full minute of flying time.

It took a long time to put the 1903 flyer together, set up the "junction railroad," and get good weather for flying. This first flight wouldn't be that easy. The first time the brothers fired up the engine to try it out, it twisted the shafts. These are what pulled the bicycle chains that turned the giant propellers. They had to wait while their old friend Charlie Taylor, back in the bicycle shop, made stronger shafts and sent them along. They were very lucky to have Charlie Taylor. He had helped them to make the motor, so he knew how to make the shafts. But the new shafts also got twisted. As winter approached and the flyer still sat untried, the brothers began to feel that time was against them.

A visit from George Spratt gave the brothers a much-needed boost. He got to witness the world record-setting glides. And the day after Spratt's departure, Octave Chanute arrived. He brought news that Langley's aerodrome had been tossed into the air in October only to flop into the middle of the Potomac River within seconds. The weather was terrible during Chanute's stay. Before leaving, he bought two pairs of gloves to send back to his young friends who stayed at Kitty Hawk as November wore on. This act of kindness was typical of the old gentleman. Orville wrote to his father about Chanute and the way he felt about the two brothers: "He seems to think we are pursued by a blind fate from which we are unable to escape." He seems to have been right.

Charlie's new shafts didn't arrive until November 20. This delay made it impossible for Orville and Wilbur to be home by Thanksgiving as they had planned. But while they waited, they began to think how they would tell the world that they had flown. Their older brother Lorin was appointed press agent. It would be his job to inform the newspapers and the Associated Press, a national press organization whose stories appeared in newspapers around the country.

When the new shafts came, they were quickly fitted on, but the sprockets were too loose. The brothers weren't so easily outdone, though. Orville wrote to his old friend Charlie Taylor: "The next morning, thanks to Arnstein's hard cement, which will fix anything from a stop watch to a thrashing machine, we stuck those sprockets [chain drive gears] so tight I doubt they will ever come loose again." Unfortunately, however, the new shafts weren't strong enough. More time was lost while Orville went all the way back to Dayton to make new, solid metal shafts. By the time he returned, it was December 11. But he did bring news of Langley's latest failure over the Potomac.

Finally, on December 14, 1903, the brothers decided that the flyer was ready for a practice run on the "junction railroad." They lifted the flyer too quickly, however, and it settled gently but solidly back to earth. They would have to do some minor repairs before it would be ready for another trial. In spite of this setback, Wilbur wrote to the family with confidence: "The machinery all worked in entirely satisfactory manner, and seems reliable. The power is ample." So the questions about the motor and the propellers appeared close to being answered. The next day, December 15, they tried again. This telegram Wilbur sent sums up the results: "Misjudgement at start reduced flight... power and control ample. Rudder only injured. Success assured. Keep quiet." The telegram operator misspelled Wilbur's name. He obviously had no idea how famous this young man would soon become.

The brothers spent much of the next day repairing the flyer and getting it ready for the next try. Christmas was almost there, and they wouldn't let their hobby keep them away from home on such an important family holiday. But it seemed that the weather would seal their fate. On December 17 the wind blew a steady twenty miles an hour. This was faster than they had intended to fly in, but they decided to go ahead anyway.

The Wright brothers must have sensed that this flight would have a great impact on history. They signaled the Kitty Hawk fishermen to look on as witnesses. They also set up the camera so that it pointed toward the end of the "junction railroad." One of the men, John Daniels, was shown how and when to squeeze the bulb in order to take a picture. Typically, both brothers were dressed in business suits and starched collars, unlike the rough fishermen who helped line the flyer up on the rail.

Orville and Wilbur had tossed a coin to see who would be the first to fly, and they agreed to switch turns each time they tried. It was Orville's turn. Barely after 10:30 A.M., with the motor roaring, Wilbur loosed the rope that held the flyer. He walked alongside it, steadying the wing as it moved down the track. The flyer moved only about seven miles an hour. Daniels was to take the picture just as it reached the end of the track. That is exactly what he did. The photograph clearly shows the first time any human being had gone into the air in a heavier-than-air, powered machine. Wilbur is standing just to the right. He seems to be looking at what he had always expected to see—history in the making!

The flyer went up in winds that were blowing twenty-seven miles an hour. It flew only 120 feet and was up for a total of twelve seconds! Orville wrote in his diary that evening: "I found the control of the front rudder quite difficult on account of its being balanced too near the center." The flyer had bumped along, going up and down, as Orville tried to control it. Minor repairs had to be made before they could try it again.

This time it was Wilbur's turn. The flight was still bumpy, but it lasted a little longer. The records of this flight aren't exact. This was very unusual for the brothers, who usually recorded every detail. It may be that they were overcome by excitement. Wilbur's flight was estimated to be about 175 feet. The third flight was made by Orville. He was hit by a sudden crosswind that caused him to turn the rudder sharply. It responded! He landed roughly, but it was clear that he had better control with this flyer than with the 1902 machine.

By noon that day they were trying the flyer for the fourth time. This flight was really something! With Wilbur flying, it went on a bumpy up-and-down course. But after a few hundred feet, Wilbur smoothed it until it reached a small sand dune nearly 800 feet from the junction railroad. Suddenly it swerved down, smashing the rudder frame. But Will and the main part of the flyer were fine. This time the brothers did measure their flight: 852 feet in 59 seconds!

The brothers' longest flight was followed by a now-famous telegram:

Bishop M. Wright
7 Hawthorne S.
Success four flights thursday morning all against twenty one mile wind started from Level with engine

The world-famous photo of the first flight by a human on a powered machine.
Orville Wright is at the controls of the 1903 Wright Flyer at Kill

Devil Hill, North Carolina, on December 17, 1903. Wilbur Wright stands near the plane.

Wilbur Wright at the controls of the 1903 Wright Flyer.

power alone average speed through air thirty one miles longest 57 seconds inform Press home #### Christmas.

Orevelle Wright

This time the telegram operator got the time and Orville's name wrong, but the message was delivered!

Lorin, the "press agent," was eating when the telegram arrived. He immediately went to the local press, which carried the story the next day. Apparently the telegraph operator, who couldn't spell either of the brothers' names right, had also managed to misinform the press. Soon there were all kinds of inaccurate and sensational news accounts floating around. Katharine sent Octave Chanute a telegram informing him of her brothers' latest victory. Interestingly enough, the Associated Press—which could have gotten correct reports to many newspapers—didn't report the flight. The Associated Press reporter didn't think a flight of less than one minute was a real story, so he failed to report it!

By December 23, just in time for Christmas, the Wright brothers had packed up their flyer, closed the Kitty Hawk camp for the winter, and returned to Dayton. From now on, they could work on improving the flyer. For the first time in history, humans had flown in powered flight!

8

"Our Baby"

The year 1903 had been an important one for the Wright brothers. During that year Wilbur turned thirty-six and Orville became twenty-nine. With $4,900 in the bank, they had enough money to feel secure. More important, they had become the first people in the history of the world to lift a powered, heavier-than-air machine into the air, fly it, and land safely.

Yet 1903 was strangely like 1900 when they had tried out their first glider. They had flown their first glider no more than one dozen times for a total of about two full minutes. But this gave them enough experience to be able to modify the glider during the following winter and improve its performance. The first 1903 flyer spent only about ninety seconds in the air over a total of four flights. But this would tell the brothers what they needed to do to improve the flyer during the coming winter. They had not yet flown a total of more than 1,500 feet on those four flights, but they were already making plans to fly over a distance of miles. They also knew that the control of the power flyer would have to be greatly improved.

There were some differences between the winters of 1900–01 and 1903–04. Both Wilbur and Orville realized that the bicycle business would have to be phased out if they were going to devote their time to improving the flyer. The cost of the 1903 machine was $1,000. This was, of course, a lot of money to them. But it was very little compared with what Langley had spent on his failed machine. Having lost $50,000 on Langley's attempts to fly, the U.S. Army would be unlikely to make another such offer anytime soon.

During the winter of 1903–04, the brothers also tried to find someplace closer to home to fly their machine. The sheds at Kitty Hawk would be closed for nearly five years before they returned to fly on the steady winds off the Atlantic. Since the flyer would now have its own power, they hoped they wouldn't need the sloping hills, soft sand, and steady breeze that had made Kitty Hawk such an ideal place.

The brothers managed to find a field called Huffman Prairie not far from Dayton. It could easily be reached by taking either the railroad or the new roads that went past it. The owner said they could use it at no charge as long as they didn't hurt the cattle he had grazing there. Early in 1904 they started building a shed on this field so they could build an improved 1904 flyer where they expected to fly it. But Milton Wright's church business again brought him under attack. Once again, the brothers dropped the work on the new flyer so that they could help their father. Family came first.

Once it was finally built, the 1904 flyer proved to be heavier than the previous one. It weighed more than 700 pounds with a man on board. But a new sixteen-horsepower engine had been built to give it more lift. Even so, the brothers faced other problems that would have to be solved before they could begin flying. Wilbur explained this in a letter he wrote to Octave Chanute:

In Kitty Hawk we had unlimited space and wind enough to make starting easy with a short track.... Here we must depend on a long track, and light winds or even dead calms. We are in a large meadow.... [I]n addition to cattle there have been a dozen or more horses in the pasture and as it is surrounded by barb wire fencing we have been at much trouble to get them safely away before making trials. Also the ground is an old swamp....

In addition, they couldn't fly beyond the field because other farmers had planted crops, such as corn, that the flyer would damage. It wasn't an ideal place for flying, but it was closer to home.

By March 1903 the brothers applied for a patent of their invention. They wanted to patent the entire idea of a powered flying machine. But their lawyer, Harry A. Toulmin, convinced them to cover only the system of controls they thought was their key to flight. It would be nearly three years before the brothers got this patent, and its limits would be sorely tested later on.

The idea of powered flight continued to interest the

readers of newspapers, and it seemed that the papers would do anything to increase their sales. Just as the reports of their flight at Kitty Hawk had been falsely reported, the brothers now found that a paper called the *Independent* had published photographs and errors. In a blistering letter to the editor of the paper, an angry Wilbur explained:

My attention has this day been called to a case of most unmitigated impudence [distorted truth] in the *Independent* of February 4 [1904].... [A]n article was published under my name which I did not write and which I had never seen.... The pictures which accompanied the article were not obtained from us, nor were they any of our photographs.

Later that year Wilbur explained to Octave Chanute: "As we have decided to keep our experiments strictly secret for the present we are becoming uneasy about—our location. In fact it is a question whether we are not ready to begin considering what we will do about our baby now that we have it." As usual, the minds of the Wright brothers were way ahead of what they were doing.

Although the brothers didn't trust the press, they realized that they couldn't ignore it completely. When the 1904 flyer was ready for its first trials, they therefore invited the Dayton press to witness their flights. But, they warned the reporters, there should be no photographs and no sensational stories. On the day of the flight, May 23, 1904, reporters came but were disappointed. There was no headwind, so the brothers had to postpone the flight until the next day. Also, the new motor was sputtering badly. May 24 was an ugly, rainy day. Only a few reporters had bothered to show up. They joined Milton Wright as he waited to see his sons fly for the first time.

The motor was still running badly, but the brothers felt that they should give it a try. The flyer lumbered down the track and struggled into a twenty-five-foot flight that ended in a landing that was both rough and damaging. To the news-hungry reporters, this was nothing to write about. But the failure may actually have been a stroke of luck for the brothers. After this, it was unlikely they would be bothered by any reporters.

The Wright brothers experimented secretly at Huffman Prairie for more than a year. But 1904 would be a learning year, not one of triumph. The next time they had the flyer ready to go, it crashed. This made more repairs necessary. By the end of June, however, they had managed flights of up to 225 feet with a total of three trips in which the flyer wasn't damaged. Two days later, however, the flyer went out of control and crashed. July and early August would prove to be equally frustrating.

Later in August the brothers made twenty-four flights. About a quarter of these flights lasted longer than thirty seconds. Huffman Prairie was a limited area, and they could go only about a quarter of a mile before they had to either land or turn around in order to stay off another farmer's field. Flying for the month ended on August 24, when a sudden gust caught the flyer and threw it roughly to the ground. Wilbur had been shaken up but was okay. All the same, it was a close call.

At about this time Orville and Wilbur were distracted by something even they couldn't ignore. The much-talked-about St. Louis Exhibition had finally begun. There would be a $100,000 first prize for the best flight. Orville and

Wilbur planned to enter the competition and had gone to St. Louis to check the flying course. Such a big event attracted worldwide attention, and flyers from Europe were also expected to enter. Alberto Santos-Dumont, a Frenchman, was expected to win the prize with his blimp. He even got the course changed to his advantage. But Santos-Dumont had trouble with his machine, and the promoters of the exhibition had even more trouble. They ran out of funds and were soon forced to close the exhibit. Luckily, Orville and Wilbur hadn't yet paid the $250 registration fee!

Now that there would be no exhibit, the brothers could devote their time to improving the flyer. To overcome the problems of taking off without a twenty-mile wind, they worked out a way to help the flyer into the air as it moved down the track. By September 15, Wilbur was able to lift off and make a true half-circle turn. The ability to turn in midair allowed him to stay up and over the small prairie. Within a week the brothers were flying beyond 4,000 feet and could stay in the air for more than a minute and a half! They were finally beating the record they had set at Kitty Hawk the previous year. Even full circles were becoming possible.

But the 1904 flyer still had problems. After this brief period of success, the brothers were again faced with a series of flights that were short and ended with damaging landings. They spent more time fixing the flyer than flying it. This year of flying ended as the last one had, in December. But while the 1903 flyer had been saved, the 1904 model was taken apart, and only the motor and transmission were saved. In recording their achievements for the year, Wilbur and Orville wrote:

During the year 1904 one hundred and five flights were made at our experimenting station, on the Huffman prairie, east of the city;...our experience in handling the machine has been too short to give any high degree of skill, we nevertheless succeeded toward the end of the season, in making two flights of five minutes each, in which we sailed round and round the field until a distance of about three miles had been covered, at a speed of thirty-five miles an hour.

As winter approached, the Wright brothers turned to family matters and their now usual business of building a better flyer. Once again, troubling church business took up much of the family's time. But Milton Wright was now seventy-six years old, and it was time for him to retire.

The 1905 flyer was assembled at Huffman Prairie and was ready for a test flight in June of that year. Wilbur wrote to Octave Chanute: "[W]e have decided to complete the machine and take the risk of making a few private trials of the improvements we have added to the machine." The new flyer was slightly longer and higher than the 1904 model. But the control system had been changed. Now the person on board would be able to warp the wings and move the rudder and the elevator separately. These changes would give the man more control over the machine, by allowing side-to-side control separately from up-and-down control. Nevertheless, the first flight with the new flyer ended quickly with a hard landing and the usual need for repairs.

The months of July and August followed the familiar pattern of disappointment and repairs that the brothers knew so well. Controlling the flyer's up-and-down movement was still a major problem, as were sudden gusts of wind. They therefore decided to try a larger elevator moved farther away from the main wings. The rudder, too, was enlarged, and the flyer behaved well. By September, Wilbur had written to Octave Chanute: "Our experiments have been progressing quite satisfactorily, and we are rapidly acquiring skill in the new methods of operating the machine. We may soon attempt trips beyond the confines of the field."

During September they were able to fly frequently and with good control. On September 17 Wilbur wrote to their old friend George Spratt: "We have been continuing the experiments with the power machine. In seven trials last week we covered almost fifteen miles altogether. The longest was a little over three miles." As the month wore on, the flights became even more successful. The brothers were now circling the field and flying figure eights. On September 26 they made a flight that lasted almost eighteen minutes with full control. They were forced to land when the fuel gave out. Even a close call with a thorn tree didn't keep them from flying.

Since their flights had been limited by the fuel supply, the brothers now added a larger gasoline tank to the flyer. The stable flyer and the larger tank worked well. By October 5 Wilbur had flown more than twenty-four miles within thirty-eight minutes. That flight broke two things— their own world record and their privacy. In response to a story reported by the *Dayton Daily News*, Wilbur wrote to Octave Chanute:

Some friends whom we had unwisely permitted to witness some of the flights could not keep silent, and on the evening of the 5th the daily *News* had an article reporting that we were making sensational flights

99

every day. It was copied in the Cincinnati [Ohio] *Post* the next day. Consequently we are doing nothing at present, but before the season closes we wish to go out some day and make an effort to pull the record above one hour.

The letter went on to invite Chanute to witness their next flight. The old gentleman came, but the weather prevented them from flying, and the machine was put away for the winter.

This season of flying would be the last the brothers had for three years. Although they continued to make improvements on the 1905 model, they had now turned their attention to another matter—finding a buyer for their machine.

9

"A Flea in Its Ear"

The idea of a dependable flying machine was something new to think about. Wilbur had written to his father in 1900 saying: "—while I am taking up the investigation for pleasure rather than profit, I think there is a slight possibility of achieving fame and fortune from it." But now that someone had proved that this idea could become reality, people had to be convinced of its value. This was the challenge the Wright brothers now faced. How would their flying machine be used—and by whom? The idea of flight was deeply rooted in the human mind. Shortly after hearing about the Wright brothers' most recent flight, Godfrey Cabot, an influential man in Massachusetts, wrote to Senator Henry Cabot Lodge at the end of 1903:

> You will doubtless have noticed in the papers an account of a successful trial of a flying machine made Dec. 17 in North Carolina by Wilbur and Orville Wright of the Wright Cycle Co., Dayton, Ohio.... [I]t showed a sustaining capacity of over 100 lbs., in excess of the weight of the operator and motor.... It has occurred to me that it would be eminently desirable for the United States Government to interest itself in this invention.

The Wright brothers themselves felt that their flyer might be useful as a means of spying on enemy movements during wartime. Perhaps, too, their machine might even put an end to war. After all, if each side knew what the other was doing, there would be no more secrets—and no more war. It was this notion that prompted them to write this letter to Congressman Robert Nevin, who represented the people of Dayton:

> The numerous flights in straight lines, in circles, and over "S"-shaped courses, in calms and in winds, have made it quite certain that flying has been brought to a point where it can be made of great practical use in various ways, one of which is that of scouting and carrying messages in time of war.... [W]e shall be pleased to take up the matter either on a basis of providing machines of agreed specification, at a contract price, or of furnishing all of the scientific and practical information... together with a license to use our patents.

The congressman's response to the brothers' letter clearly showed, however, that the U.S. government did not understand the value of their invention: "[T]he Board has found it necessary to decline to make allotments for the experimental development of devices for mechanical flight." It was also clear that the government's memories of the money it had wasted on Samuel Langley's failed machine had made a stronger impression than did the success of the Wright brothers' flight.

When the brothers' offer to the U.S. government was turned down, they realized that they would either have to find another buyer or give up on the value of their invention. But they were faced with two problems. First, they would have to put a price on their work. Second, what if they found a foreign buyer and were no longer viewed as loyal Americans? There are many letters in which the Wright brothers expressed how deeply they were concerned about this matter of loyalty to their country. A letter Wilbur wrote to Octave Chanute summed up the brothers' feelings: "We have no intention of forgetting that we are Americans, and do not expect to make arrangements which would probably result in harm to our native country."

Still, there is no doubt that the brothers were bitterly disappointed in the reaction of the U.S. government. Late in May of 1905, just as they were beginning construction of a new flyer, Wilbur wrote to Octave Chanute: "We are only waiting to complete arrangements with some government. The American government has apparently decided to permit foreign governments to take the lead in utilizing our invention for war purposes.... [So] we have made a formal proposition to the British Government." A speedy reply from Chanute stated: "As an American I greatly regret that our government has apparently decided to allow foreign governments to take the lead in utilizing your invention." He went on to question whether the right people knew about the brothers' offer. Since he was known in high government offices, Chanute thought he could attract the interest of the War Department. He therefore asked the brothers, "[W]ould [you] object to my putting a flea in its ear?" But they had been stung by the government's rejection and decided to make their offer to the British as planned.

The British had been trying to master flying on their own, so the Wright brothers' inquiry did spark some interest. They had been following the brothers' work for several years. In 1904 they sent Lieutenant Colonel John Capper to see Octave Chanute. Capper then went to Dayton to see the Wright flyer. Of course, he wanted to see it in flight. But fearing that their ideas would be stolen, Orville and Wilbur were only willing to show him photographs of earlier flights. By the summer of 1905, however, they were more interested in doing business with the British. Wilbur explained their thinking:

> It is no pleasant thought to us that any foreign country should take from America any share of the glory of having conquered the flying problem, but we feel we have done our full share toward making this an American invention.... It has for years been our business practice to sell to those who wished to buy, instead of trying to force goods upon people who did not want them.

In March 1905, therefore, the Wright brothers offered to produce a flying machine that would carry two men for fifty miles without stopping for fuel. They would demonstrate the machine in England, being paid for the miles it flew. If the flyer went the full fifty miles, the British government would pay them $125,000 for it. When a

British government official visited Dayton, however, he found that the brothers were willing to demonstrate the flyer only after a contract had been signed. The brothers were smart businessmen as well as great inventors. With so much work ahead of them, and the promise of such a large amount of money, they closed their bicycle shop for good that summer. From now on, their job would be selling the flying machines and the idea of flight.

By October of 1905 the Wright brothers' success had become public knowledge, especially after the *Dayton Daily News* story broke. But the British still hadn't responded to their offer. A British colonel was supposed to visit them while on business in the United States, but he hadn't shown up yet.

Meanwhile the French had become interested in the brothers' ideas. Octave Chanute had spoken to a group in France during the summer of 1903, telling them about the gliders Orville and Wilbur had made. Then, in 1905, the Wright brothers were offered a chance to compete for a $10,000 prize in a flying contest in France. But they turned down the offer. Both the French and the British were trying to build their own flyers. Why risk having their secrets get out for so little money? the brothers asked themselves.

Shortly after that, an offer to buy a Wright flyer came from a Frenchman named Ferdinand Ferber. But the French were clearly questioning how anyone could have flown without the whole world knowing all about it. Also, how could the brothers have accomplished so much with so little money? Who had sponsored them? Surely the two bicycle makers couldn't have done everything on their own!

While both the British and the French waited, the

brothers continued to work on their 1905 flyer. At the same time, Octave Chanute was still trying to convince them to make their offer to another U.S. government official. They finally wrote to the secretary of war in October 1905:

> Some months ago we made an informal offer to furnish the War Department practical flying machines suitable for scouting purposes.... We are prepared to furnish a machine on contract... the machine to carry an operator and supplies of fuel, etc., sufficient for a flight of one hundred miles... at a speed of not less than thirty miles an hour.

Again the War Department failed to understand that this was not an experiment the Wrights wanted funds to conduct. They were turned down again.

This time the brothers sent reports of their flying successes to the three countries they thought would have the greatest interest in flying: Britain, France, and Germany. Stories of their work had been published in the leading magazines of all three countries. The British believed the reports, but both the French and the Germans questioned them. Representatives from both countries were sent to check out the Wright brothers' claims. Orville and Wilbur still refused to demonstrate their flyer in action. But the French were so impressed that they offered to buy a Wright flyer for 1 million francs. This was nearly $200,000 in U.S. money. The brothers would be rich! But an offer wasn't a reality. The terms of the contract ended without the promised money. However, Wilbur and Orville Wright did make $5,000 as part of the arrangement even though the contract fell through. This would keep them going while they made other attempts to sell their flyer.

What followed were long months of frustration. The British failed to pursue the Wrights, thinking that their own attempts at flight would succeed. They didn't. The United States also failed to make an offer the brothers could accept. It appeared that the United States would only make an offer once the idea of powered flight was accepted. How could two men who wanted to protect their invention prove to their own government what they could do if they refused to fly in public?

Even the intervention of Senator Henry Cabot Lodge of Massachusetts didn't succeed in urging the U.S. government on. In a letter to Godfrey Cabot, the Wright brothers explained: "We are ready to negotiate . . . but as the former correspondence closed . . . [it appears] the board did not wish to be bothered with our offers, we naturally have no intention of taking the initiative again."

In a letter to Octave Chanute, Wilbur explained why the brothers were willing to wait for a good offer:

> If it be assumed that some one else will produce a practical flyer in a year or two years at the most, or that by refusing to buy, governments can force us to sell at their own terms, then the price we ask is undoubtedly too high. But if the governments know that there is only one way to get a practical flyer within five or ten years, and then there is no hope of beating down the price, then they will consider the price very low. . . . Even you, Mr. Chanute, have little idea how difficult the flying problem really is.

Parts of this letter clearly acknowledge the efforts of others in at least three other countries to learn how to fly. Added to that number were several in the United States, including Alexander Graham Bell, who had earlier invented the telephone. But these efforts were meeting with no real success at that point. In spite of their patience, the Wrights weren't getting anywhere in their attempts to sell what they had invented. They therefore accepted the offer of Charles Flint to represent them in Europe while they had exclusive rights to sell in the United States. Soon there was talk of a $500,000 deal and a private flight as a demonstration for the czar of Russia. But this never took place.

While they waited for new developments, the brothers worked on an improved motor. In the spring of 1907, Wilbur explained to Octave Chanute: "Our newest engine just completed gives more than 30 horsepower, or 50% more than we used in our 1905 flights. It is enough power for two men, fuel, and a hundred pounds of extras." That same spring, Flint claimed that he was making progress. He asked one of the Wright brothers to come to Europe to meet politicians and investors who could help sell their flyer. They decided that Wilbur would go, and he boarded an ocean liner on May 16, 1907. First he went to London, where he was outfitted in tailor-made clothes so that he would be dressed to meet important people. With talk of vast sums of money coming from the sale of the flyer, Orville wrote: "I would give three cents to see you in your dress suit and plug hat!"

During the following months there would be a whirl-wind of activity, but no results. This was also the first time that the brothers were separated for such a long time. It wasn't easy for them to communicate with each other, and they missed this. In the bicycle shop they only had to look at each other to know what the other was thinking. Now there were costly telegrams, called cables, but these were very slow. Wilbur went as far as Berlin, the capital of Germany, to find a government that would buy their flyer. The negotiations and delays caused a strain between the two brothers for the first time. But by mid-June, an almost unexpected buyer was expressing interest—the U.S. government. The brothers had never fully given up wanting to sell the flyer to their own country.

There was so much going on in Europe, however, that Orville and the mechanic Charlie Taylor joined Wilbur there. During this time Wilbur, ever the writer, wrote an article for *Scientific American* called "Flying as a Sport—Its Possibilities." It drew a great deal of attention to the brothers and their flying.

While they were together in Europe, the brothers saw the sights, and Wilbur wrote to Katharine: "I stopped to look at the inside of the Notre Dame. It was rather disappointing as most sights are to me. My imagination pictures things more vividly than my eyes." Somehow that wasn't surprising. After all, this was someone who had invented powered flying. In a letter to Milton Wright, Orville summed up their activities by saying: "We have been real good over here. We have been in a lot of churches, and we haven't got drunk yet!" The brothers also spent time observing the attempts at flight being made by various people in Europe. They felt confident that their idea was still safe.

With fall approaching, the travelers decided that it was time to return home. Orville and Charlie went first, followed a few weeks later by Wilbur. On his return from the docks of New York, Wilbur stopped in Washington to work on the U.S. offer. To avoid accusations of unfair secret deals, the government required that there had to be open competition for the contract. In the "Advertisement and

Specifications for a Heavier-Than-Air Flying Machine" the government called for a machine that could carry two men at forty miles an hour for one hour and return them safely. The Wrights' bid would be $25,000, far less than they had first asked. On February 10, 1908, the Wrights signed a contract with the U.S. Signal Corps. But they were also finishing another contract with the French. They received an offer of nearly $140,000 for the flyer they would provide. On March 3, 1908, they agreed to form a company in France, pending an acceptable demonstration of the flyer.

With 1908 approaching, the secret of flight was being discovered by others—and the Wright brothers knew it. A Frenchman named Henri Farman had recently flown for seventy-four seconds. By 1908 others would be flying for several minutes—up to six and a half at a time. The work of Alexander Graham Bell's group continued in the United States. Perhaps it was time for the brothers to return to Kitty Hawk.

10

"I Wish I Could Be Home"

Two of the men associated with Alexander Graham Bell were Glenn Curtiss and Lieutenant Tom Selfridge. The lieutenant wrote to the Wright brothers at the end of 1907, asking for specific information on how they controlled their flyer. Thinking that the request was being made for research purposes, the brothers sent him a detailed reply. This was the beginning of many problems they would have with the Bell group.

By 1908 the reality of human flight was clearly being accepted by many people. The competition among flyers was also growing. The business value of it was becoming known as well. Wilbur had explained to Octave Chanute how he and Orville viewed it: "We do not wish to get into lawsuits before we get the business properly organized and started. Our plan is to spend the winter building a half dozen new machines for the spring trade. We do not fear any competition until after we show our machine."

But the competition continued. Bell's group had built a new flyer with a Curtiss engine that flew 319 feet. Another Bell flyer flew more than 1,000 feet by the early spring of 1908. This was the first serious American competition the Wright brothers faced. By April of 1908 the new Wright flyers were coming along, and it was time for one brother to go on to Kitty Hawk to prepare it after three years of absence. The 1905 flyer had been modified to seat two people, and new steering had been added. As the older brother, Wilbur went ahead. He had the usual problems getting there with all the supplies and the huge crates in which the flyer was packed. When he arrived, he wrote to Orville: "I reached K.H. [Kitty Hawk] last evening.... This morning I went down to camp and found everything in ruins."

Knowing that 1908 would be a demanding year, Wilbur wasn't happy about all the work he would have to do to get the camp into shape. As if this weren't enough, the press knew that he was there to fly. Soon many papers were carrying stories about the remarkable flights he was making—yet he was still on the ground! He wrote to his father: "This is my eleventh day from home and only one day's work has been done on the new building.... Just before noon yesterday Charlie Furnas showed up. I was not particularly glad to see him." Charlie was the mechanic from Dayton who had been sent to help. Orville had already been asked to delay his arrival.

It was early May before the first flight of 1908 could be made. It lasted for twenty-two seconds. It was necessary to get used to the new steering system. Small trial flights were made, while the press continued to report stories of incredible flights. Orville, by now at Kitty Hawk, wrote to Katharine: "The flight was not quite equal to that described in the Norfolk papers a week ago, probably not $1/200$ as long." But these stories sold newspapers, and this was what the press wanted.

The brothers' main goal that summer was to fly with a passenger on board. They had agreed that the two of them shouldn't go up together in case there was a serious crash. Orville wrote to his father in May: "Yesterday morning [14th] we tried carrying two men for the first time. Will made a flight of about 500 ft. with Chas. Furnas on board .... A little later I took him a complete circle...in 3 minutes and 40 seconds." That afternoon Wilbur was still fighting the new controls. The result was a hard crash into the soft sands of the Outer Banks. Orville called it "a big splash of sand." Wilbur was shaken up. The reporters, who were hiding not far away, had a great story to tell! The brothers didn't like having them around and weren't very nice to them. As Wilbur explained: "It is a good thing sometimes to have a fierce reputation, like a school teacher."

The brothers had a lot to do that summer, and they were behind schedule. Then a telegram arrived saying that one of them would have to go to Europe to work on the French contract. The U.S. contracts, too, would soon demand their attention. Predictably, it was Wilbur who went to Paris. He hoped to be able to finish the work there quickly and get back in time to help Orville.

Wilbur arrived in Europe on May 29, 1908. There he faced two European flying firsts—an eight-mile flight in France and a two-man flight in Italy. Were the Wright brothers falling behind the Europeans? Wilbur set about finding a safe place to make trial flights, while Orville

113

packed a flyer and sent it to him. The distance separating the brothers caused tension between them. In June, Wilbur wrote to Katharine: "I have no word from Orville since leaving Kitty Hawk. Does he intend to be partners anymore?" When he finally heard from Orville, it was only to receive the crate that had been sent. Wilbur wrote to his younger brother: "I opened the boxes yesterday and have been puzzled ever since to know how you could have wasted two whole days packing them. I am sure that with a scoop shovel I could have put things in within two or three minutes and made fully as good a job of it.... Did you tell Charley [Charlie Taylor] not to separate anything lest it should get lonesome?" The damaged flyer would take longer to assemble than Wilbur expected. Orville would have to go to Washington, D.C., alone.

With five flyers in production, trial flights for the U.S. Army coming up, and people constantly peering in at the windows to watch him, Orville had his hands full. Wilbur added more to this workload by promising that they would write an article for *Century* magazine. In explaining why he had done this, he told Orville: "[W]e need to have one true story in an authentic way at once and let it be known that we consider ourselves fully protected by patents. One of the clippings which I enclosed intimates [suggests] that Selfridge is infringing on [using without permission] our patent on wing twisting [warping]." Orville, who had never enjoyed writing, would have to do this important piece alone.

In Europe, Wilbur, too, was hard at work. He was living in the shed near the flyer and staying away from the many parties to which he was being invited. He took in a stray dog as his only close friend and named it Flyer. But he had problems when the water-cooled engine overheated, throwing scalding water on his arm and burning him badly. However, he assured Katharine: "[M]y burns were not very serious.... I had a 'docteur'... probably a 'hoss doctor,' come to dress my arm.... I fired the 'docteur' after his first visit."

Orville had many things to worry about, including his old friend Octave Chanute. He wrote to Wilbur: "Chanute had an article... criticizing our business methods, and saying we have always demanded an exorbitant [too high] price." Orville later replied about their old friend after another article: "[H]e again criticizes our business methods... but we have gone to the other extreme.... He says the use of the flyer is greatly overestimated, generally, and that its uses will be very restricted." Many other letters showed the brothers' concerns about their patent, which had not been issued until May 22, 1906.

By now it was August 1908, and Wilbur had to work on filling the conditions of the French contract before it expired. The city of LeMans was buzzing with excitement. On August 8 Wilbur made one short flight there, but it was enough to show how steady and maneuverable the flyer was. Two thousand people came for the next flight. Before long the crowd had increased to 3,000. Wilbur described the outcome to Katharine: "All question as to who originated the flying machine has disappeared. The furor has been so great as to be troublesome. I cannot even take a bath without having a hundred or two people peeking at me.... I do not like such conditions."

Meanwhile Orville had to go to Washington, D.C., to take care of the contract with the U.S. Army. The competition was open to others who could meet the conditions, and the brothers' old enemy, Augustus Herring, was there. Orville got the flyer ready ahead of the deadline. But

Washington was like LeMans when it came to people's interest in flight. Even the president's son came to watch. Orville wrote to Katharine: "I haven't done a lick of work since I got here. I have to give my time to answering ten thousand fool questions—about the machine." Neither of the brothers liked being in the public eye. Even though they were 4,000 miles apart, they seemed to be having the same experience. They were being peered at by people on both sides of the Atlantic—and they were both equally disgusted. While Orville was complaining to Katharine, Wilbur wrote to Orville, saying simply: "I wish I could be home."

Orville was soon ready for his trials. But he wasn't happy about Bell's two men, Glenn Curtiss and Lieutenant Selfridge, being there to witness the flights.

In the meantime in Europe on September 6, a Frenchman set a record of nearly one-half hour in the air. All the same, Orville created a real sensation in the United States. Orville flew for more than an hour, and Washington nearly emptied so everyone could see him fly. He broke his own records time and again, flying one hour and fourteen minutes—and up to 310 feet high! But he wasn't finished yet. It was time to meet the conditions of the army contract at Fort Myer outside of Washington. Orville now had to fly with two men on board, and of all people, Lieutenant Selfridge was selected! On September 17, 1908, the flyer struggled to get into the air, but it did. Then something "popped" and was thrown loose. Horrified, Orville found that he had no controls. The flyer slammed into the ground before several thousand people. This was their worst accident yet. The flyer had to be pulled off the two men. Orville suffered a broken leg and ribs, and had to be carried away. Lieutenant Selfridge wasn't so lucky. He died shortly after the crash.

As always, the Wright family drew together. Katharine left her teaching job to care for her brother. She never left him during his entire six weeks in the hospital. Old Charlie Taylor had been at the crash and simply broke down when he saw one of "his boys" so badly hurt. It turned out that one propeller had split and cracked in two, causing the crash by breaking through the steering lines.

Wilbur didn't rush home to his brother's side. Apparently he felt that he had to fly in order to prove that the flyer was safe. He explained to Katharine: "The death of poor Selfridge was a greater shock to me than Orville's injuries.... I felt sure 'Bubbo' would pull through.... Tell 'Bubbo' that his flights have revolutionized the world's belief regarding the practicality of flight. [The press now] accept[s] human flight as a thing to be regarded as a normal feature of the world's future life." Wilbur himself would make more than 100 flights at LeMans. More than half of these would include passengers. In describing the huge crowds and the impact of his flights, Wilbur wrote: "One old man of 70 living about 30 miles away made the round trip [to see me fly] on a bicycle every day for nearly a week."

Praises were being heaped on the brothers from every side. Milton Wright, who was usually very reserved, wrote to Wilbur: "You and Orville are, however, secure... in the temple of fame. 'Conquerors of the air.' Its extensive results are, as yet, uncomprehended and undreamed of, even by yourselves." Octave Chanute, despite his criticism of the brothers, added: "I congratulate you heartily upon the magnificent success which you have achieved in

Wilbur Wright and a passenger on a 1909 exhibition flight in southern France.

France—and upon the prospect that you will reap a fortune from your labors."

By December the U.S. Army's contract had been extended because of the accident, and Orville, with Katharine, went to Europe to join Wilbur. By the end of the year, Wilbur had flown almost ninety miles in more than two hours. It was clear that the brothers were now well ahead of any other flyers. And to prove it, business was booming. They sold flyers and training to those who could afford it. In Rome, they received an offer of $10,000 for a Wright flyer. While there they met and flew before King Victor Emmanuel. The awards, dinners, and honors were numerous. After Orville had returned home, Wilbur

118

wrote: "The government [of France] had decided to confer upon me the 'Legion of Honor' but—I sent word that it would be impossible for me to accept an honor which Orville could not equally share."

By now it was the summer of 1909, and the army's contract still had to be filled. The brothers had found time to improve their steering, and a new flyer was sent to Washington. There were the usual problems, including a minor crash from which Orville walked away unhurt, but by mid-July the flyer was ready. Even President Taft came to watch as Orville set and broke his own records. During one flight he flew for one hour and twenty minutes and went as high as 300 feet. On July 31, with President Taft and his cabinet among the crowd, Orville prepared for the speed trial. He would have to fly ten miles at 40 miles an hour for the $25,000 contract. If he went faster, $2,500 would be added for each additional mile per hour. Of course, if he went slower he would lose $2,500 for each mile he lost. The crowd waited breathlessly when the plane flew out of sight. After fourteen long minutes it was back— at an average speed of 42.5 miles an hour! Earlier in the day Orville had beaten the one-hour record with a passenger by staying up for seventy minutes. At long last, the U.S. Department of War had signed a $30,000 contract for Wright flyers.

While Orville captured the world's attention in Washington, Wilbur continued to dazzle Europe. When the world's first international air races were held in France during the month of August, the only airships entered were Wright flyers they had sold earlier. The brothers felt no need to compete, choosing to let the flyers they had built do the competing. A new world endurance record of three hours in the air was set before a crowd of one-third of a million people. Following the races there were two air crashes in which the pilots died. One of them had been using a Wright flyer. The other pilot was the Frenchman Ferdinand Ferber. The brothers were sad to see pilots they had trained die in such a way.

The only American to enter the races was Glenn Curtiss, who was served with papers for patent violation by the Wrights while he was in France. Their attorney, Harry A. Toulmin, had gotten patents in all the European countries that were sponsoring flight. The Wright brothers were therefore covered in Europe as well as in the United States—or so they hoped. Wilbur was called to Berlin on German business. Orville, along with Katharine, joined him there in August. They met Kaiser Wilhelm, emperor of Germany and king of Prussia, and saw huge German blimps. Then Orville showed off the Wright flyer with a flight that lasted more than one and a half hours and went as high as 1,600 feet.

The Wright brothers were growing tired of the crowds and the constant attention, however. Wilbur, finally back in the United States, had to go to a huge celebration held in New York. Glenn Curtiss had been invited as well, and he came. The Curtiss flyer had been having problems. But Wilbur wowed the huge crowd by doing an unscheduled flight around the Statue of Liberty. When Curtiss couldn't perform or fly, Wilbur made a twenty-five-mile trip up and down the Hudson River before a crowd of about 1 million people! When he landed, he announced that it would be his last public flight. He just wanted to go home.

The brothers had earned some time off. The Wright Company, backed by some of the richest men in the United States, was formed, promising $100,000 in cash plus stock and a share of sales for the two brothers. Among the

Orville and Wilbur Wright in France.

investors was J. P. Morgan, one of the nation's wealthiest men. Wilbur, naturally, was the president and Orville the vice president. Before 1909 ended, however, the brothers had to go to court in the case of *Wright* v. *Curtiss*. They won the first case on their patent, but it was appealed, and more cases continued to come along. These court battles continued for years.

As if the brothers weren't having enough trouble, their old friend Octave Chanute again questioned their claims in the press. He even went so far as to challenge them on the invention of wing warping. Early in 1910 Wilbur wrote a pointed letter to his old friend. In it he reminded Chanute that what Chanute had recently been saying in the press was very different from what he had said when the brothers first made this invention in 1901.

Octave Chanute replied:

I did tell you in 1901 that the mechanism by which your surfaces were warped was original with your-selves.... [B]ut it does not follow that it covers the general principle of warping or twisting wings: the proposals for doing this being ancient.... If, as I infer from your letter, my opinions form a grievance in your mind, I am sorry, but this brings me to say that I also have a little grievance against you.

Wilbur fired back another sharp reply. But Chanute, in his late seventies, was on his way to Europe, where he fell ill and died on November 23, 1910. Over the years Chanute had been a good and valued friend to the younger men.

The rest of the 1910 flying season was spent on business. The company had settled in Dayton and contin-ued to use Huffman Prairie to experiment with new ideas.

Wilbur had seen his fill of flying and never flew there. But Orville, ever the daredevil, made about 250 flights. It was here that he finally took his brother Lorin up. Charlie Taylor, too, got his first flight there. So did the brothers' beloved father, who, at age eighty-one, loved it!

In 1911 and 1912, a Wright Flyer Model B was produced. Flight was now so widely accepted that a newspaper offered $50,000 to the first flyer who could go across the United States in less than thirty days. The brothers had no time to devote to this newest challenge, however. More and more of their time and effort went into lawsuits to protect their ideas. When court cases were tried in Europe, it was Wilbur who went.

When it was time for the brothers to spend some of the money they had made, they decided to build a new family home. Orville would work on that while Wilbur was away. He selected a twelve-acre site in the expensive area of Oakwood, south of Dayton. The house would be named Hawthorn Hill. Wilbur, of course, had to have some say from Europe. "In looking over the proposed plan of the new house...I see plainly that I am going to be put in one of the south bedrooms so I propose a new plan for them. In any event I am going to have a bathroom of my own, so please make me one."

Wilbur kept up his exhausting pace, never content to rest. He wrote three articles telling the true story of Otto Lilienthal and others. On his return to the United States, more business took him to New York and then to Boston. By May of 1912 it was clear that something he had eaten had made him ill. But he had to see the Model C flyer the company was now working on. Then he had to see where the new house would be. Finally he went back to 7 Hawthorn Street, but he remained busy. The illness took his

This 1910 photograph shows airplane wings inside the Wrights' shop.

appetite, and Katharine called a doctor. It was typhoid fever, and it was very serious. In bed, Wilbur dictated his will. His brother Reuchlin came from Kansas, and the others drew near. Wilbur was forty-five, and it soon became clear that this was a challenge he would not win. On May 29, 1912, the man who had stood on the beach near Kitty Hawk and watched his brother sail into the air for twelve seconds died quietly in the beloved family home on Hawthorn Street.

Even at his advanced age, Milton Wright still kept a diary. In it the loving father summed up his famous son: "In memory and intellect, there was none like him.... He could say or write anything he wanted to. He was not very talkative. His temper could hardly be stirred.... He could deliver a fine speech, but was modest."

11

The Kitty Hawk Flyer

Wilbur's death had a tremendous impact on Orville. For the first time in his life, he couldn't look forward to asking his older brother questions and having them answered. The first thing he did was to see that Wilbur's last wishes were carried out. He wrote to his oldest brother, Reuchlin: "I think it was Will's wish to have the Wright Company interests stay in my hands. I am sure it is the desire of the other stock-holders. I do not think there is any question about our winning our patent suits, but, of course, there is no certainty in the law." Milton Wright agreed with Orville and wrote to Reuchlin: "Concerning Wilbur's will, it is his last testament. Every one of us wants it carried out in every particular, as if it were a sacred writ. His will was that each brother and his sister should have fifty thousand dollars. Orville regards the will as if sacred, and will carry it out precisely."

The first matter of business was having Wilbur buried as he had wished. He joined his mother in the family plot, leaving room for his father and the others when their time came. Then there was a company to run. Orville became president of the Wright Company, which continued to grow as Wilbur had expected. There would be a British Wright Company Ltd. (Limited), as Wilbur had been expecting. Then there was a victory in the German courts in which the brothers' patent was upheld. Both Orville and Katharine traveled to Europe for these events.

In March 1913 it began to rain in Dayton, and it didn't stop for many days. With the Miami River on one side and Wolf Creek on another, the water began to rise. Orville wrote to a friend in England:

> The water covered over half the city.... On Hawthorn Street it was about eight or nine feet deep and stood six feet on the first floor. Most of our things downstairs were ruined.... During the time of the highest waters fires broke out in different parts of the city and nothing whatever could be done to stop them.... We have been without regular street car service, electric light and gas for the past four weeks.

The Wrights' greatest loss was hundreds of photographs that had been taken to show their progress in flight. Many negatives were damaged by the water. Other parts of the Wright property, however, were more lucky. Their Oakwood home and the Wright Company's factory were on higher ground and remained untouched by the flood. The business carried on. At the end of 1912 the company had produced the Wright Model C, but it didn't do well.

For the first time, Orville had failed to keep up with the competition. The biggest American competition came from Glenn Curtiss. His company tried new designs, such as moving the propellers to the front of the wings and adding pontoons to land on water. Orville didn't make changes like these. It wasn't that he didn't think about changes, though. While he was devoting his time to making the flyer more stable, the newest airplanes were being designed with cockpits. The pilot wouldn't be out in the wind anymore. His invention didn't work with the new Curtiss planes.

The court cases involving the Wright patent continued, and by 1913 Orville had won a major victory. But he was thinking about selling the business. He wanted to dedicate his life to telling the Wright story and securing the brothers' place in history. In June 1914, however, the brothers' invention faced another challenge from Glenn Curtiss. He managed to get the 1903 Langley flyer from the Smithsonian Institution. Samuel Langley had been splashing in the Potomac River while the brothers were preparing to fly at Kitty Hawk. What Curtiss did was to redesign the flyer and get it into the air for a matter of seconds! On May 28, 1914, the press was invited, and a 180-foot flight occurred. Then A. F. Zahm of the Smithsonian stated that the original Langley flyer was capable of flight *before* the Wrights' plane flew. Such a finding would challenge the Wrights' ownership of their patent. This was Curtiss's way of getting even for the lawsuit he had lost.

To Orville, much more than the patent was at stake. The Wright brothers' place in history was being challenged illegally. As a result, the Langley aerodrome would hang in the Smithsonian labeled the first flyer in history! The year 1914 held more surprises for Orville, however. He bought an automobile so that he could drive the few miles from Oakwood to the Wright Company. He also began to plan a sale of the company, since Europe seemed to be on edge of war. World War I broke out later that year.

The United States didn't enter the war for three years. But when it did, many new airplanes were needed. As late as June 1917, Orville still expected flying machines to end war. He explained: "We thought governments would realize the impossibility of winning by surprise attacks, and that no country would enter into war...when it knew that it would have to win simply by wearing out its enemy." He was wrong. Trench warfare was the rule during World War I. In addition, the newest Wright models had performed poorly, and too many pilots were dying in crashes.

It was 1917 when the United States joined the war. In April of that year, Milton Wright went to bed one evening and failed to show up for breakfast the next morning. Orville's beloved father had died in his sleep. He was placed beside his wife and Wilbur in Woodland Cemetery.

Perhaps to cheer himself, Orville brought home a Saint Bernard puppy that he named Scipio. In no time the puppy outweighed Orville! But Saint Bernards aren't long-lived dogs, and Scipio came down with painful joints and limped around. Orville knew how the dog felt. Ever since the crash in which Lieutenant Selfridge died, he had had a bad back and needed to wear a special belt. Scipio and his master became fast friends. As the family grew smaller, Orville found himself more in need of such companionship. His oldest brother, Reuchlin, died in 1920.

Orville found one source of pleasure in a summer place he had bought on the Canadian side of Lake Huron. It was there that he learned that Katharine would get married. The ceremony was held at Oberlin College, where she had gone to school and where she had first met the man she was marrying so many years later. But in 1929 Katharine, too, fell ill and died of pneumonia. Except for a loyal servant and Katharine's husband, who were like family to him, Orville was now alone in the huge house. He was often tempted to give up, but he had the family name to live up to. He couldn't stop yet. The Langley affair had never been settled, and the 1903 flyer he called the *Kitty Hawk* was getting old as it sat in storage. The Dayton flood ruined many things, but the *Kitty Hawk* had survived. With its place in the history of aviation unclear and Langley getting credit for something he did not do, Orville decided to send the flyer to the Science Museum in London on loan. There it would not have to compete with the false Langley claim. It was shipped January 31, 1928.

Monuments to the Wright brothers were numerous, and the world continued to heap honors on them. One monument was placed on Big Kill Devil Hill. There are three hills there, so the tallest was used for the monument. A new airport in Dayton was named Wright Field. A Wright Memorial Bridge now spanned Currituck Sound from the mainland to the Outer Banks. The Hawthorn Street house had been abandoned, and the bicycle shop had not been used for years. Henry Ford bought both of these buildings and had them moved to Greenfield Village in Dearborn, Michigan. Greenfield Village is a collection of houses and factories from before World War I that Henry Ford assembled. A university in Dayton was named Wright State. It is where the largest collection of the brothers' papers can now be found. A magnificent museum in Dayton was also dedicated to the Wright brothers and their accomplishments.

But Orville felt that he and Wilbur had been cheated

Orville Wright and Henry Ford at Hawthorn Hill in 1936. Ford moved the Wrights' Hawthorn Street home and their bicycle shop to his museum at Greenfield Village in Dearborn, Michigan.

of the biggest monument of all. Proper recognition of their unique contribution hadn't been given to them by the most respected institution of its kind. The Smithsonian still accepted Curtiss's claim that the Langley aerodrome had made the first powered flight in history. Orville may have felt that he had let Wilbur down. In 1928, however, a leading scientist, Charles G. Abbot, became head of the Smithsonian Institution. He realized that the Langley claims were based on Curtiss's later flights. Finally, in print for all the world to see, the Wright brothers' claim was recognized in 1942 in a story Charles G. Abbot wrote. By then World War II was raging, jets and bombers wreaked havoc, and the *Kitty Hawk* was stored underground in England so Hitler's bombs wouldn't destroy it. On the fortieth anniversary of the *Kitty Hawk* flight, it was announced that the flyer would be brought home. But it had to wait for the war to end.

When the war ended, plans were made to bring the flyer home. It would take a long time to get there, though. Orville, who was now in his seventies, felt as if he, too, had been freed at last. The family's name had been cleared, and he could now take a rest. He didn't live to see the *Kitty Hawk* come home, however. He died of a heart attack on January 31, 1948. He was laid to rest near his beloved brother Wilbur, his father Milton, his mother Susan, and his sister Katharine.

On December 17, 1948, forty-five years after its flight, the heirs of the Wright brothers gave the *Kitty Hawk* to the Smithsonian Institution. The Wright brothers are long gone, but what they left lives on. Today you can see the memorial near Kitty Hawk, visit Wright State University and the museum in Dayton, and tour the Hawthorn Street

The 1903 Wright Flyer known as Kitty Hawk *at the Smithsonian Institution's Air and Space Museum in Washington, D.C.*

house and bicycle shop at Greenfield Village in Dearborn, Michigan. The Wright brothers' gift to humanity can also be seen with each rocket and airplane that flies. But perhaps most important of all, you can visit the Air and Space Museum in Washington, D.C. In 1976, during the U.S. bicentennial, the museum was dedicated as the newest addition to the Smithsonian Institution. As you go into the front door, you will see, hanging overhead grandly, in the main lobby as the most prized display, the *Kitty Hawk* flyer. It is frozen in flight forever.

Important Dates

1867 Wilbur Fiske Wright is born on April 16.

1871 Orville Dewey Wright is born on August 19.

1874 Katharine Wright is born.

1878 Milton Wright brings his sons a toy helicopter.

1889 Susan Koerner Wright dies from tuberculosis.

1892 Orville and Wilbur attend Chicago World's Fair; the Wright brothers open first bicycle shop.

1896 Orville very ill from typhoid fever; Otto Lilienthal dies in a glider crash; during 1896 Samuel Langley begins secret flight experiments.

1899 Wilbur writes to Samuel Langley about flying.

1900 Wilbur takes first trip to Kitty Hawk; Orville joins him later. The 1900 glider flights start in October.

1901 Wilbur and Orville return to Kitty Hawk on July 10 to test 1901 glider. They stay until August 22.

1902 Wilbur and Orville leave for Kitty Hawk in August and return October 31.

1903 Wilbur and Orville return to Kitty Hawk with 1903 flyer in September.

1903 Orville Wright makes history's first powered flight on December 17. Later the same day Wilbur flies 852 feet in 59 seconds.

1904 Wright Flyer II makes first full circle over Huffman Prairie on September 20.

1905 Wilbur and Orville write to Senator Nevin offering to sell aircraft to the U.S. Army; the offer is refused. Wright brothers close bicycle business to sell flying machines instead.

1907 Wilbur Wright sails to Europe to sell flying machines.

1908 Wrights sign a contract with U.S. Signal Corps to build and deliver a flying machine. Wilbur returns to Kitty Hawk. Orville soon joins him. New flyer designed for two and extra weight.

1912 Wilbur dies on May 29 at 7 Hawthorn Street from typhoid fever. He is buried in Woodlawn Cemetery, Dayton.

1914 Glenn Curtiss "flies" redesigned Langley aerodrome on May 28; claims Langley aerodrome was capable of flight before the Wright flyer.

1917 Bishop Milton Wright dies in his sleep at Hawthorn Hill. He is buried in Woodlawn Cemetery, Dayton.

1928 *Kitty Hawk* is sent to London for exhibition.

1948 Orville dies of a heart attack on January 31; he is buried in Woodlawn Cemetery, Dayton. The Wright brothers' estate gives the *Kitty Hawk* to the Smithsonian Institution for display forty-five years after the first powered flight.

Bibliography

Andrews, John Williams. *First Flight* (a narrative poem). Westport, Conn.: Pavilion Press, 1963.

Brown, Aycock. *The Birth of Aviation.* Winston-Salem, N.C.: The Collins Company, 1953.

Crouch, Tom. *The Bishop's Boys.* New York: W. W. Norton and Company, 1989.

Hallion, Richard, ed. *The Wright Brother's—Heirs of Prometheus.* Washington, D.C.: Smithsonian Institution, 1978.

Howard, Fred. *Wilbur and Orville—A Biography of the Wright Brothers.* New York: Ballantine Books, 1987.

Kelly, Fred C., ed. *Miracle At Kitty Hawk.* New York: Arno Press, 1972.

McFarland, Marvin W., ed. *The Papers of Wilbur and Orville Wright.* New York: McGraw Hill, 1953.

McMahon, John R. *The Wright Brothers, Fathers of Flight.* Boston: Little, Brown, and Company, 1930.

Meynell, Laurence W. *First Man To Fly.* London: Werver Laurie, 1955.

Taylor, John R., supervising ed. *The Lore of Flight.* Gothenburg, Sweden: Tre Tryckare Cogner & Company, 1970.

Walsh, John E. *One Day At Kitty Hawk.* New York: Thomas Y. Crowell Company, 1975.

Wright, Orville, edited by Fred Kelly. *How We Invented the Airplane.* New York: David McKay Company, 1953.

Index

About the Author

Richard M. Haynes is the Director of Field Experiences and Teacher Placement and Assistant Professor in the Department of Administration, Curriculum, and Instruction in the School of Education and Psychology at Western Carolina University. This is his sixth book. Dr. Haynes writes primarily history books, often centering around North Carolina history, and most often for young adults. He and his wife, Dianne, and their daughters, Lisa and Heather, live in Waynesville, North Carolina.